Silence of the Lad, Why Men Stop Talking

What Men Need to Tell and Women Desire to Know!

Anthony X. Page

Silence of the Lad

All Scripture quotations, unless otherwise indicated, are taken from the HOLY BIBLE: Holman KJV Study Bible Copyright © 2014 by Holman Bible Publishers, Nashville, Tennessee. All Rights Reserved

Printed in the United States of America

ISBN: 978-0-578-33012-9

DEDICATION

I dedicate this book to all the voiceless men who live in regret. To the men who because of trauma, felt that hiding and cloaking in shame was your only solution.

I dedicate this book to the little boys confused by labels, segregation, and misunderstanding, stop seeking to become what God said, instead acquiesce.

I dedicate this book to the husbands who never knew that loving your wife is impossible without loving yourself first.

I dedicate this book to all the men and women who will read this book, and your eyes will be open to see how you contributed to silencing your son, your brother, your uncle, your husband, and your father, and you will decide to be better!

I dedicate this book to all who will make the decision to no longer live in the regret of your past but step into a new day.

Now that you know better, be better!

ACKNOWLEDGMENTS

To my mother, Alice D. Page, thank you for believing in me and pushing me into destiny. You are a big part of my story. Had you not been my rock, compass, and constant cheerleader, I don't know how I would have survived. I'm so glad you got to see your prayers answered and the transformation occur. I know me being your pastor was one of your great joys, but you being my mother was God-ordained! I am glad you had the opportunity to see my transformation from silent and docile to bold and expressive. I miss you terribly but know I will see you again. Rest well, apple of my eye.

To my siblings, Denise & Marcus Page, thank you for allowing me to tell my story with you included in portions of it. We had an eventful upbringing, one definitely filled with love and a lot of shenanigans. Mom was our rock and taught us how to stick together and rock out for each other. You both are indeed the wind beneath my wings!

To the greatest churches in the DMV, Face2Face Worship Center, thank you for allowing me a platform to fulfil my call and use my voice. Week after week, you afford me the privilege of doing one of the things I love most, preaching and teaching God's word. You all are a stellar group of people that I'm honored to serve. Now let's continue to pursue destiny.

To the men and women who allowed me to interview you and share your transparency. Your stories help collaborate my perspective on why the male voice is needed in our relationships, communities, and society; men cannot stay silent. And to all those who help edit my book. Your review, feedback, critic, and suggestions were crucial to helping me make it over the finish line! I Salute You!

To my Pastor, Bishop Ken Chism and the other men and women of God who have encouraged and undergirded me on this journey and who continued to push me to excellence, your presence in my life is God-ordained and I honor each of you.

To my greatest creations, Alexandria Taylor and Rhylan Cecil. You both have grown to be beautiful women inside and out. Your kind, generous, and loyal dispositions are a hallmark of how your mother Rhonda raised you. You both make me extremely proud and committed to never stop striving to be a father who is present emotionally, vocally and physically. Thank you for loving me and helping me to break the generational curse of male silence. Your need for my voice continues to motive me to never stop speaking life! Ladies you are my heartbeat!

Finally, to Dennard Mitchell, and NL Publishing, thank you for coaching, mentoring, and providing the information, guidance and partnership needed to write my first book. You are definitely an inspiration to many. I pray I can inspire others as you have me and our book writing challenge group! Continued blessings and continue to Soar "big brother" Soar!

FOREWORD

Society has presented a strong agenda of male versus female and who is the greater or lesser of the two. Truth be told, if we were to pay attention to history, the impact from the male voice has been influential and set the tone for the greatest of movements. Dating back to the book of Genesis, when God Himself spoke things into existence, so it became. It became because it was voice-activated, which shows the importance of having a voice and speaking out. He didn't just internalize a thing; He spoke it and spoke to it!

Over time, the family structure in many homes has changed. Which, in a sense, has had an impact on the way many men have been taught to react and respond. Statistics show that more males are being raised by single mothers because of the absence of the father, which has a major effect on the household and how males view themselves. When men are not present, it causes a break in the structure of the family. In some instances, the lack of male presence has left many men questioning their leadership capabilities, their self-esteem, and self-worth as well as their very own existence. The male presence and what he speaks is a chain reaction to how he feels. Speaking up and speaking out should be a dominant trait; whether introverted or extroverted, it all matters.

The voice of the male carries weight which, if not handled properly, will pressure men into thinking if they're not vocal enough, they're powerless, and their masculinity is questioned, or if they're too vocal, they're competitive. However, if males are voiceless and silent, there is a possibility that there are other issues far greater than just not having anything to say. Often a male's silence represents the frustration he may feel or suppress feelings and emotions that have never been dealt with.

Some men have been taught to shelter their feelings instead of being complete and whole in their thought process because it makes them feel less than if they were to speak up and it is not received. Some think silence shows strength, while being vocal shows one's weakness in certain situations. When a male goes silent, their thoughts are being challenged, and silence can imply that the situation won't change as long as nothing is added to it, when in reality, the voice and power that the male possesses, with the strength of God, will change what was into what is, according to God's will and purpose.

This book, "Silence of the Lad, Why Men Stop Talking," will guide, counsel, and equip men to know the power of their voice. As Anthony takes us through his own experiences, you will discover what men have to say is important when it comes from a pure place far beyond arrogance and pride. The voice of men is a key component to rebuilding, empowering, uplifting and changing lives. It is time for us as men to break the silence and speak up. To silence the man is to silence a generation.

Bishop Kenneth Chism, Restoration House, International,

TABLE OF CONTENTS

INTRODUCTION

Why was Adam silent when the serpent approached Eve in Genesis 3:1-7? The Bible says that after Eve was deceived by Satan, she took of the forbidden fruit, ate it and then she gave some to her husband, who was there with her. The scripture makes it plain that Adam was there with Eve the whole time. But why didn't Adam say anything?

Before God created Eve, He had already commanded Adam not to eat from the tree of the knowledge of good and evil. Adam was to pass this command to his wife, who was made from his side. Eve, bone of his bone and flesh of his flesh, Adam was to profess, to protect and to provide for her.

But when the serpent approaches Eve, and starts a conversation with her, challenging God's goodness and commandment, Adam says nothing. He listens to every word and even hears Eve misquote God's command concerning the forbidden tree, which we assume he shared with Eve. Adam hears Satan in his crafty way contradict what God said, but Adam is silent. He watches as Eve begins looking at the forbidden tree. He sees her walk towards the tree and reaches out to take fruit from the tree. And Adam didn't do a thing or say one word to stop her. Adam remained silent! Why?

Adam said nothing. He stood there, heard, and watched the

whole thing and didn't say a word. He failed his wife that day. He failed to profess, protect and provide for his wife.

The silence of Adam is the beginning of every man's failure, from the silence of Abraham concerning revealing Sarah's real identity to King Abimelech, the struggle of Jacob and accepting a label given him from a circumstance he had no control over, to my silence that ultimately brought about the demise of my marriage. It is a picture, although disturbing but a revealing one - of the nature of our challenge as men. That if not intentionally resolved and refined, may result in the failure of our relationships, the demise of our character in society and the ugly legacy we leave for generations of men that follow. When men are silent, it affects the entire world.

Since Adam, every man has a natural inclination to remain silent when he should speak. Men, as we were created, are most comfortable in situations where we know exactly what to do. But what happens when men don't know what to do. When men are scared, confused, unable to solve the problems of their families, provide for the love of his life or answer questions about the future. His chest tightens, his voice goes mute, and he backs away in fear. When life frustrates him with its unpredictability, trauma pushes him to hide, and answers seem elusive. What does he do? Seek counsel in the safety of the multitude, talk and reason with his wife or significant other or escape to the most familiar place, the place most natural since his creation, the place of silence?

The book you hold in your hand will examine this condition that many men struggle with, SILENCE. Is it a natural inclination from Adam, our first father, or a result of something experienced in the formative years of your life? A trauma, a generational curse, a labeling that makes it easier to hide rather than wrestle for identity.

We will explore male silence, its impact on male identity, on male and female relationships, and the impact it has on families and society. We will discuss what a man can do to regain his voice and how a woman can assist in the conversion. We will also present for consideration, remedies derived from personal experiences, interviews of individuals affected by male silence, and ultimately, what guidance the scriptures offer.

Men, as chronicled in scripture, were uniquely called to remember what God said and to speak accordingly, to move into unchartered territories with confidence and wisdom that comes from listening to God, remembering what He said and acting on it!

Chapter One
My Why

Chapter One

MY WHY

"Silence creates a barrier that blocks real intimacy."

When we fail to talk, giving expression to our feelings, our thoughts, and our hearts, we distance ourselves from the people we love and from the God who can heal. It is said that intimacy is defined as "in-to-me-you-see." But intimacy occurs through communication, verbal and non-verbal.

When we remain silent, we give power to our fears, cement our issues, and create a self-imposed prison.

When we open ourselves up and begin to talk, to share, to express, we break the barriers that imprison us, and the healing of our spirit can begin.

I wrote the above paragraphs in my journal at a very pivotal time in my life. I had been married for about two years, and seeing the frustration, disappointment and shear hurt in my wife's eyes caused me to go into self-reflection, realizing that I had created a world of emotional hurt in her because of my silence. I was probably like a lot of men in their relationships and marriages, a silent partner.

The adage is that "silence is golden," but at that point in my life, I had to ask myself what was golden about me not having a voice, not participating emotionally in my marriage that was beginning to starve due to the lack of verbal attention and heartfelt communication? Not realizing until this point, I was a man who had lost his voice and didn't know it. My silence, my non-responsiveness and my aloofness in the relationship with my wife and others were customary. It was my normal.

Where did this tendency, this behavior come from? What or who made me like this? I was at a crossroads that required investigation, understanding and possible intervention. Specifically, what was it that really made me tick, operate in the manner that I did?

Now before I go into the details of the why for my silence, the how it occurred, the effects of this behavior in my relationships and my ultimate conversion from a silent partner to a participatory communicator, I must share with you what it is you currently hold in your hand, whether you're reading from the paperback book or your smart device. I want to share what this book is and is not.

I want to be explicit in first stating, this book is not a mission to solve the mammoth crisis of what I call **"male silence."** As I stated in the introduction, this problem has been around since the creation of mankind. The silent male behavior was passed down from our first father, Adam, as we saw in Genesis 3:6

We will absolutely explore this dilemma to seek an understanding of how, why, and what men want to share with the women we love and the people we are in a relationship with, how we view communication and what is necessary to assistance, and maybe even support us in moving from the place of silence. Please pay close attention because you don't want to miss the keys that will be shared to assist men in going from voiceless and silent to voluble and communicative.

But I want to be clear in my intentions. This book is my story, how my voice was lost, how I became voiceless, as I now call it today. It is my hope that my story will provide another lens from which to view **male silence**, how it happens for many, what are ways to manage or understand it, and more importantly, to realize the beauty of your creation as men and speaking spirits.

When a person aligns themselves with the purpose of God, that God created every human being with the ability to speak, articulate and express through the medium of their voice, you begin to understand that your voice is one of your most powerful tools, instruments even, which God gave us! Your voice gives you the power to create. All who are reading, understand that your world is framed or created by your words. Could you not have the world you desire because you have created the world you do not want with your negative, self-defeating, self-condemning words? One of my favorite scriptures states this principle, Proverbs 18:21:

"Death and life are in the power of the tongue: and they that love it shall eat the fruit thereof."

As this biblical principle reveals what you eat or experience in life, relationships, your finances, your perspective, is a result of your words, what you have spoken! Look at your words as seed, each word you speak is a seed, and when a seed is planted, it brings forth fruit. What fruits are you producing with your words?

Are you producing life, encouragement and hope with your words or are you producing discouragement, doubt, and fear? I encourage you, even challenge you, as you read this book, begin to take an inventory and **ask yourself the following questions**:

- Are most of the words I use to express myself negative?
- My self-talk, does it always focus on what I cannot accomplish?
- Do I encourage others with my words?
- Do I discourage others with my words?
- Do I magnify the negative aspects of a situation and filter out all the positive ones with my words?

If you answered three or more of these questions in the affirmative, or as you thought about your answers to the questions, did you identify a trend, a tendency? That you use more negative words or view things from a negative perspective more than you do a positive perspective. I have some news for you. You are seeing the seeds of your words. You do know that words come from thoughts and thoughts produce actions. If I've just described you or perhaps caused you to wonder if it's you I'm talking about. Yes, you're the person I'm talking to and about, no need to guess any longer … you're the person. I've come to challenge you, to push you, to provoke you. Check the words that are coming out of your mouth. Here is your opportunity to change your world through your words.

Before I proceed with my story, I want to ask you to do something for me.

Take a moment and consider what makes you silent or renders you voiceless in the affairs of your life as a man? When life occurs and unexpected circumstances happen that are not necessarily favorable. Difficulty arrives; a failed marriage, a job loss, defiant children, a spouse who doesn't believe in your dreams, a boss who criticizes your performance. The vicissitudes of life present themselves and your response is silence. Is silence a default for you? Do you find it easier to be silent because silence helps you maintain a neutral position or does your silence lend itself to pseudo peace, a type of calm that absolves you of any responsibility or accountability for your life?

Is that you or perhaps you know someone who fits the description. If so, I want to challenge you, encourage you, find your voice, or give this book to the person you know in an effort to help them! What areas of your life have you either become silent or have never spoken?

Are you present in your society, in your children's lives, in your relationships, for yourself? The real truth is that your voice gives you a presence in your world. I want to invite you to view this book from the lens of this being a counselor's couch upon which you can rest yourself, in the safety of your own thoughts and absences of others criticism. Begin to identify, confront, and address your muteness. Isaiah 1:18 admonishes

"Come now, and let us reason together…"

Men, our women need us present, physically, spiritually, and most importantly, vocally! Our communities need us talking, reasoning, and facilitating healthy dialogue that will bring change and advancement for our people.

Could the genocide in our communities, black-on-black crime, men killing men and women, result from us as men not talking or being willing to talk and communicate? Have we settled for fighting it out with our fist instead of resolving it with our words? I believe every man reading this book can start from here and begin to do things differently. To identify your voice, to begin using the creative tool given to you by God to build the best world for your family, your society, and most importantly yourself. I believe every woman who reads this book has an opportunity to create a canvas, an environment in which your man can find safety in your presence to talk and express himself without judgment or ridicule, to be vulnerable and intimate, where for the first-time woman, ***in-to-him-you-can-see***.

Now, please understand you will not get a psychological diagnosis of men. I am neither a trained or licensed psychologist nor an expert on what makes men talk. Although I am a certified relationship counselor and licensed/ordained Pastor who have counseled both men and women as it relates to relationships issue and counseled men individually on a plethora of areas, including the challenge men have with being the men they were created to be, their God defined identify. However, I do not write from the perspective of a man who is perfect or has mastered the art of communication. I, however, write as a man who suffered many years with silence and muteness. I believe that sharing my story from the terrain of my life and all its intricacies and traumas, will help other men to know that they can be free from the silence that binds them.

Consider men and women, some view male silence as a phenomenon that has yet to be solved. I say that in sarcasm understanding that often, when something is said in sarcasm, there are elements of truth sprinkled in the statement.

In doing research for this book, I came across many books, articles, blogs, and periodicals psychoanalyzing men. Specifically, in an effort to understand how we communicate, our communication patterns, styles, and the reason behind our often misinterpreted and misunderstood silence.

In the abundance of material published, attempts were made to identify male silences. Some of the answers provided were:

- *We don't talk about emotions and feelings because talking about our feelings may make us appear effeminate or less-than masculine, and we fear that when we do talk about feelings, the female or other males may view us differently, i.e., as weak.*
- *The safe option is for us is to remain silent, which prevents being labeled and viewed as less masculine.*
- *We often feel that we cannot win or might not get heard if we share our feelings. We might feel we have less vocabulary or that we might lose the argument.*
- *We are silent because if we share and are misunderstood, we might get angry and do something we should not do. Ultimately believing that silence helps maintain order and control.*
- *We hurt when we see the female in our lives upset and specifically if we can't figure out how to solve a problem for them, so we retreat into silence.*

The validity of the reasons varies from man to man. However, the truth is silence impedes on the progress of any relationship and prolongs destiny fulfilment. Silence breeds misunderstanding, isolation, and barriers to connection. When men remain silent, they give power to their issues and create the potential to repeat the cycle.

*"***When you don't have a voice, you can't stand up for yourself.***"*

What you will find in this book:

o My personal journey that caused my silences and lessons learned during my formative and early adulthood.

o Testimonies of men and women sharing how **male silence** affected their lives and perspectives on the importance of the male voice.

o Life principles that will aide other men in finding their voice and becoming strong communicators in every sphere of their lives.

o Guidance for women in helping them to understand the power of the male voice, the order established by God for the male voice and how the family benefits when a man speaks.

Are you ready for the journey? Why don't you grab a cup of coffee, tea, soda or whatever your favorite drink may be? Find a nice cozy spot in your living room, bedroom or like I often do, go to one of your favorite restaurants where you can hang out for an hour or two. Get a nice booth, and prepare to be humored, enlightened, and prayerfully inspired to find your voice as men. Women, if you've picked this book up as a possible holiday or birthday present for your man, do yourself a favor, read it first yourself.

In this book, you will find some valuable nuggets that either you weren't aware of about male silence and/or how you can become a catalyst for change. You just might find some helpful tools that you can use to assist and encourage your man, who seems to always be silent when you need his input and voice the most. You need him to speak to transform from a place of being saturnine, sullen, and disconnected to engaged, participatory and expressive.

My prayer is that my personal story will help men of all walks of life, vocations, colors, and creed; identify your voice and begin to walk in the power and genius of your voice. Men, your voice speaks to your identity and the authority given you by the Creator. Your voice releases your original creativity - the why God created you male. Men, it is our time to remember what God said and to speak!

~ The Journey Begins ~

~ Questions For Reflection ~

1. Take a moment and reflect WHY do you think you were born?
2. Are you waiting on someone to tell you your WHY?
3. Have you asked God WHY you were created?
4. What will you do with God's answer to your WHY?

Chapter Two
THE BEGINNING!

Chapter Two

THE BEGINNING!

"Kids are to be seen and not heard"

In life, the power of our voice is so crucial and pertinent to not only a person's survival but their identity as well. We often don't realize how necessary our voices are until we're placed in a situation where we need to speak and can't. I grew up in a home where my father was military, and my mother worked in the federal government. It was, I venture to say, a typical middle-class African American family. My two siblings and I were close emotionally and in age range. Each one year apart in age and our perspectives on life are primarily the same. My sister, the oldest, has a very nurturing temperament, and my brother, the adventurous one. My mother spent a lot of time teaching my sister to cook, clean and basically look out for my younger brother and me.

We grew up in what would today be characterized as a strong male chauvinistic environment. We grew up to understand there were specific roles for men and women, and they were different. The things my sister did in the home were labeled as "what women should do," and my brother and I were programmed to think men's work was to do anything "outside of the house," i.e., cut grass, take out the trash, and fix cars. However, the one caveat my brother and I had to clean the bathroom toilets because that job was "too nasty for a woman to do." We also had to make up our own beds every morning upon rising from sleep.

Growing up in the Page household, these defined male and female roles and responsibilities were ingrained in our psyche and for the most part, the roles and responsibilities did not cross-pollinate. My father, a man who was a stickler for order and structure, impressed upon us, each gender had specific roles and responsibilities, and if they crossed, it would contradict their gender identity. This principle was so ingrained during our formative years that when my sister or mom would ask or try to get my brother and I to wash the dishes or do what was deemed as "what women should do," my father would adamantly object and we didn't have to do the chore. Growing up in this manner was actually a delight for my brother and I. We never had to worry about washing the dishes, cooking, laundry, or things of that nature. Maybe that is why today I still do not cook well. This dogmatic teaching, however, would prove toxic and not healthy as my brother and I grew older and experienced the world. This teaching propagated toxic masculinity and skewed our view of male and female roles.

My father had a strong physical presence in our home. Although he was not a strong disciplinary nor very affirming or affectionate, we grew up knowing who wore the pants in the home. My father was neither very verbal. He wasn't one big with words. When he wasn't drinking alcohol, he was fairly quiet and docile. He didn't provide a lot of instructions or guidance when telling us what to do. My father loved women, and anytime he saw an attractive woman, he would express his thoughts without shame and with great verbose. My mother would often share with us that our father was a good provider and that although he didn't express his love or affirmation verbally, "he was a good man who paid the bills."

Growing up as little children, we didn't necessarily want for anything materially, always having a roof over our heads - never being set out on the street, and from what I recall, we always had food on the table and clothes on our backs. I would say the biggest thing we missed was our father's affection. But mother overcompensated for that. She would always shower us with loving affirmations, hugs, kisses and would play with us. I don't recall a time when my father would play ball, trucks, or anything with us. Around the age of ten or eleven, my parents moved us into our first and only family home, a three-bedroom brownstone in upper Northwest DC.

It was the first time my siblings and I had our own bedrooms, well, almost. My brother and I had to share rooms, but we were elated because we had bunkbeds from which we could jump off the top bunk and pretend we could fly. My sister was the oldest and therefore had her own bedroom. We felt like we had died and gone to heaven. Unlike when we lived in the apartment where the three of us shared a bedroom, life was good for the Page kids. Not only did we have our own bedrooms, but we had a fenced-in backyard that we would play in after school and on the weekends.

It was during that time that we would often hear my father say when at the dinner table eating and my siblings and I attempted to voice our opinions or thoughts, my father would cut across us mid-sentence and, with a stern expression on his face say, *"kids are to be seen and not heard."* Although this phrase seemed harmless to us as kids at the time, it would later prove to be a self-defaming expression that muted us. Interesting as I recall those times and look back at my siblings and myself today. I think this expression impacted my brother and I greater than my sister. We ended up being muted because my father was muted. He was a silent voice in our home.

My mother, in comparison, was a talker. She was not shy nor docile at all. She was an opinionated woman who freely spoke her mind. Before giving her life to Christ, it would be commonplace for mother to use expletives with every other word. I recall one time my father saying to my mother, "Peaches, why do you curse at the kids so much." Peaches was my mother's nickname from my father. Even though he said that to her to correct her behavior, it didn't make a difference. Mother had a thing for expletives. I share this to make a point. My father was mute, and my brother and I subliminally began to mimic his example, whereas my sister was the opposite. She mimicked my mother's expressive, talkative nature.

There is a prevailing principle that I think is worthy of taking note of. Parents with young children, you may not always realize it, but your children learn through watching your behavior. What children see displayed repetitively, they will begin to repeat. Psychologists call this behavior "imitating adults."

Parents, when you recognize inappropriate behavior from your children instead of reprimanding them, take inventory of your behavior and what you may have said or displayed around them. Take this opportunity to consider your ways and adjust your behavior. Remember, in the formative years, your children are sponges, and everything they see, hear and what happens around them will influence their behavior and develop their identity.

In hindsight, it was not usual that my brother and I grew up to be silent men. Voiceless in relationships, in our environments and ultimately where it mattered the most, silent within ourselves.

As I look back over those early days, what did the phrase "*kids are to be seen and not heard*" mean? What was it I heard as a little boy? In processing it now as an adult man, I believe it was then that I internally began to believe that my words, my opinion, and my voice didn't matter. It was in these formative years as a little boy I learned to muffle my voice. Actually, I learned to silence my voice! In silencing my voice, I also began to silence my thoughts, believing that my thoughts had no value, no credence! As a little boy, the silencing of my voice mushroomed into me silencing my emotions. In my young mind silencing my emotions, I believed it prevented me from being rejected. I remember a specific time as a little boy when I had fallen and scraped up my knee really bad. I came home crying and expecting the comfort of my mother. To my dismay, I ran into my father and the words he spoke to me would forever be seared in my mind, validating my need to silence and hide my emotions. My father said to me, "*men don't cry.*" I remember quickly wiping my eyes and burying my emotions within myself.

My father's words taught me to hold back my tears even when they needed to flow, to avoid expressing my true feelings because others might reject me or view me as weak. This would eventually lead to a greater level of fearing rejection and the need to fit in. The interesting thing about fear is that when it settles into our spirits, it creates torment and gags our emotions and feelings. The Bible describes the power of fear in this way; 1 John 4:18

"... fear hath torment."

Interestingly, when examining the word torment in Greek, it means to torture, harass, or be distressed by. I grew up tortured by the prospect of rejection, and therefore, what became my safety zone was silence. "*But perfect love casteth out fear.*" The answer to my dilemma of silence was love, unconditional love. Like many before me and after me, I was a little boy looking for his voice but convinced I didn't have one.

As I remember the words my father spoke, "*Kids are to be seen and not heard*," that phrase materialized in many other ways than just during childhood. It would affect my adolescent, teenage, and early adulthood. I would grow to be a man not having a voice. It was also during this formative time that we learned how to perform. It's funny because in my father telling us that "*kids were to be seen and not heard,*" the statement proved to be inaccurate to what he expected from his kids. Let me explain. When my mother and father would have parties and invite some of their close friends and family over to our home, it would never fail. They would wake my siblings and I up from sleep in the middle of the night and have us come into the living room where the party was going on and the music was booming loud. Whether Wilson Pickett, Smokey Robinson or the Parliament-Funkadelic's was playing on the stereo, we'd jump on the dance floor in our pajamas, whip the sleep from our eyes and go to moving to the rhythm of the beat, entertaining the adults.

Ironically, we were children who loved to dance, to move to the beat of the music. It was apparent that our dancing amused our parents, and the performance was such that they would want other adults to see us dance, perform at their beck and call. What was the message, the underlining principle or lesson?

We learned a very important principle, one that would follow us for the rest of our lives. We learned the importance of performance, that if you perform to the standard and expectation of others, you will be accepted and receive the applause of others. This is a lesson I didn't realize I was learning until I look back forty years later. My siblings and I learned to perform, that the right performance will garner you the applause and accolades of people. It will make you popular and you will feel accepted. Although we were constantly told we didn't have a voice, if we performed to the standard expected, we could have a presence, an audience! We learned first-hand as children what we would later define as pretending! We learned how to act right and look right.

Appearance seemed to be everything. Looking the part was strongly emphasized. This was one of the mantras of our home. We couldn't leave the house without being appropriately dressed. My mother or sister never left the house with rollers in their hair or what they called "house clothes," i.e., pajamas and house slippers in the street. My father always had creases in his pants and shoes shining like new money. We had to be dressed appropriately and presented well any time we stepped outside the house.

I believe this is why today I am so meticulous in my appearance.

Everything has a place and must always be in its proper place. When something is out of place, my rhythm is thrown off and my disposition is agitated. This was the home I grew up in. I don't share this to brag that our home was better than other homes but submit, this was probably the culture in many middle-class African American homes.

I share this point also because I believe the impression imprinted on my psyche as an impressionable little boy carried into adulthood. It was from this perspective that we learned to judge and be judged by esoteric factors. Factors that didn't really matter or fortify us in the natural world or the world to come.

Not realizing it, our parents taught us to be great performers, wear masks, look the part, and act in a way that allowed us to fit in or subscribe to a specific image, an image that we didn't determine or choose but one that was conferred upon us. By whom? Society, the fashion industry, religious beliefs, etc. It's interesting because we grew up thinking that we should look like the family on the church fan when we went to church. We had to dress a certain way, act a certain way when in public. And not that those things were bad in and of themselves, however what they taught us was performance and image were more important than having a voice and knowing our authentic self.

Think about it. What are we teaching our children? Are we teaching them how to be performers, wear mask, fit an image, play the dress up game, while minimizing or never really understanding the power of their authentic voice? Interestingly, as a little boy growing up, those were the subliminal messages taught me. Those were the messages that my siblings and I grew up learning.

I don't believe our parents intended for us to grow up, to focus on presentation more than our identity. But that was our experience. I write this book in an effort and hope to help those who will read these words become aware that it's not about your performance as much as it is about your identity. Are you heard? Do you feel that your voice has power? Do you feel that you have a valid voice? A voice that would bring change to an environment, warmth to the heart of those you love as well as insight and wisdom to a conversation.

The power of your voice - I write this book with hopes that men will regain their voice. Man, where did you lose your voice? Was it when you were a little boy and bullied by your classmates? Was it when a family member molested you, and you told no one for fear of ridicule and labeling?

Was it when you were a teenager, and no one paid attention to you or devalued what it was you said? I want you to follow me as I chronicle my story and examples of men throughout scripture who lost their voices. As we investigate these lives together and see how they regained the power of their voice, my hope is you will gain the confidence to recapture your voice.

My brother, you are in a safe place, and your secrets will not be judged. You are not alone on this journey but surrounded by a cloud of witnesses cheering you on. I, like you, was a silent lad, a little boy voiceless, afraid and lost. But if I can regain my voice and walk in my God-designed destiny, so can you! God is no respecter of persons and what He's done for me, He will do for you. You have made the first step; you are reading this book. As you read paragraph after paragraph, begin to see yourself as vibrant, vocal and vociferous.

The world is waiting on you. You have something to say. How do I know? Because you are still here! What was intended to kill you will **now reveal you**!

~ The Wrestle ~

As shared, my silence began in my formative years, but it also infiltrated into my early twenties and thirties until I had a reckoning with myself and God, a wrestling likened to the one Jacob experienced described in Genesis 32:24-28. Jacob had to come to terms with who he was named, labeled, identified as - simply based on a situation he had no control of. His story narrates the details for us who he was created to be, but in order for that to happen, an identity conversion needed to occur - a name change would be necessary! God would call him to a place of transformation, but it would not be without a struggle.

So Jacob was left alone, and a man wrestled with him till daybreak. When the man saw that he could not overpower him, he touched the socket of Jacob's hip so that his hip was wrenched as he wrestled with the man. Then the man said, "Let me go, for it is daybreak. "But Jacob replied, "I will not let you go unless you bless me. "

The man asked him, what is your name? Jacob," he answered.

Then the man said, "Your name will no longer be Jacob, but Israel, because you have struggled with God and with humans and have overcome." (NIV)

Jacob reminds me of myself in that who he was named, labeled, had nothing to do with who God called him to be. He was labeled by a circumstance beyond his control. Genesis 25:21-27 tells the story explicitly:

And Isaac intreated the LORD for his wife because she was barren: and the LORD was intreated of him, and Rebekah his wife conceived. And the children struggled together within her; and she said, If it be so, why am I thus? And she went to inquire of the LORD. And the LORD said unto her, Two nations are in thy womb, and two manner of people shall be separated from thy bowels; and the one people shall be stronger than the other people; and the elder shall serve the younger. And when her days to be delivered were fulfilled, behold, there were twins in her womb. And the first came out red, all over like an hairy garment;

and they called his name Esau. And after that came his brother out, and his hand took hold on Esau's heel; and his name was called Jacob: and Isaac was threescore years old when she bore them. And the boys grew: and Esau was a cunning hunter, a man of the field; and Jacob was a plain man, dwelling in tents.

Isaac and Rebekah named the boy Jacob, his name meaning "supplanter" in the Hebrew. The word "supplant" means "to overthrow by tripping up -- to supersede by treachery." In fact, if you study Hebrew, the name "Jacob" literally means "heel grabber." No, I'm not making any of this up; this is what the Bible teaches.

This labeling or naming of Jacob because of his circumstance - grabbing his brother's heel during conception. This one incident would imprison him. Jacob would spend his entire life wrestling, wrestling with his brother, wrestling with his father, wrestling with his mother. He had to even wrestle for his wife. But ultimately, he would have the wrestle of his life, one that would transform his thinking about himself. He got into a wrestling match with God, where he wrestled all night.

In this wrestling match, I submit to you. God was after something. He was after how Jacob saw himself, how he postured himself. His posture was a direct result of words, words that were spoken over him, words that he came to own and accept as his own.

Jacob's story was my story. I too, wrestled. I wrestled with identity. I wrestled with silence. I wrestled with intimidation and low self-esteem, all because of hearing phrases with immature ears.

Phrases like:

"Kids are to be seen and not head." "Stop acting so weak."

"Men don't cry." "Shut up no one wants to hear what you have to say."

These phrases as a little boy I internalized, and they muted me. As Jacob was robbed of his identity, I was robbed of my voice, my ability to express myself. My muted condition made me afraid to voice my opinion, share my thoughts, defend myself. I was vulnerable and afraid. I remember getting into physical altercations at school with other boys my age and older. I would be afraid to go home and tell my father for fear of retribution. And if bruised during the altercations, when I got home and my father asked what happened, I would lie and say I had fallen at school or on my way home.

I remember vividly one incident when after accepting the Lord as my personal savior at the age of twelve, my brother and I were in the car with my father at a traffic light. At the intersection, a nun proceeds to cross the street. My father began to make vulgar remarks about the nun, asking if my brother or I would have sexual intercourse with her. Now, of course, he didn't put it in those nice terms. But I remember sitting in the car thinking, why would my father say such crass things about this holy woman? I recall my brother chiming in and saying, "yea, dad, I would do her." But me, I never opened my mouth.

The reason the incident is so vivid in my mind is because it wasn't what occurred in the car that day that stuck in my memory, but what occurred later that night at the dinner table. As we were sitting around the table eating as we regularly did as a family, my father said something to my mother in the presence of my sister and brother that made me want to disappear into the floor beneath me. As the food was being passed around from person to person to get their serving, my father said, "Peaches" (*my mother's nickname*) **I bet you Tony's stuff is so clean we could eat it for dinner.** He was making reference to my genital, mocking my desire to be saved and specifically chaste.

As my family laughed, I sat there feeling and thinking what was wrong with me, why wasn't I like my brother, why didn't I speak up and chime in like my brother did, just to get along and praise from my father. I desperately desired my father's affirmation, a kind word, a fatherly hug, a sign of acceptance. But it would never fail. I would always be disappointed because he was a man of few words, and when he did speak, it would be to either curse at my mother and my siblings and I, or make sexually suggestive remarks to my brother and I about women. I would later find out from my mother that my father didn't know how to affirm us. My mother would say to us, "your father doesn't speak much, but I know he loves us because he pays all the bills."

Now, if you are of the baby-boomer generation, most likely the aforementioned statement that my mother shared concerning my father not speaking much is probably not a surprise to you. This was the typical behavior of the fathers in that day and time. It, however, did not alleviate my desire to have my father affirm and talk more to me. Those times of his silence made an imprint on my heart. I can remember my mother always coming to console and reaffirm me. Her voice was one that made me feel safe and reassured. She believed in me and would tell me as often as she could how special a little boy I was and that I could accomplish anything I set my mind to.

Like Jacob, I wrestled. I wrestled with my circumstance and labels and resolved it was best that I remain silent, absent, not present. It is so amazing how the mind works because it was also during this time that I learned to use my imagination, to daydream. It became my coping mechanism, a type of escapism. I would imagine that I had a father who loved on us and talked and played with us regularly. I would find myself telling people when they asked about my family, I would package them in such a way that my life sounded like a story book, a sitcom, liken to the Jefferson's, or the Brady Bunch. *Note: the Cosby Family was not on television when I was a little boy growing up.* I would watch those family shows and dream and imagine that my life was as perfect as displayed on television.

I write with the realization that many men wrestle in silence. Men wrestle with the labels society places upon them. Men wrestle with being good providers, husbands, fathers, and men of integrity. But men also wrestle with the question, how do I accomplish all of this when I haven't had teachers, role models, examples to show me? I have counseled several men who, in their transparency and frustration, have stated that they don't know how to be good fathers, good husbands, good men because they haven't seen it model before them. Their fathers weren't present in the home or either their fathers were silent, indifferent, or not emotionally engaged.

When hearing this from church members and clients, I initially thought it was just an excuse for negligence, that they just didn't want to take responsibility and accountability for their actions or the lack thereof. But in hindsight, I realized in our black community, we have a generation of men, baby-boomers and older men who have been silent in our teaching and training the millennials and the generation x. We haven't met the men at the point of their needs. We haven't extended the olive branch. This book is the olive branch.

The epiphany I had in counseling these young men was that *"silence perpetuates silence that ultimately manifest itself in hypocrisy."* One of the characteristics about men, when we don't know something, for shame of ridicule, and embarrassment we will keep silent, not express, not share. Let me give you an example: How many times have you women been riding in the car with a man and he gets lost, he no longer knows where he's going. Have you noticed he will not ask for your help or assistance, much less drive to the nearest gas station to ask for directions? Thank God for the invention of GPS; had not that been invented, some of us would still be driving around lost. But seriously, what this reveals is in our silence, we start pretending, masking, even hiding.

I will address silence more in-depth in a later chapter, but today is the day of reckoning for us as men. We can no longer hide behind closed mouths and quiet opinions. As Jacob wrestled with God and the result was a conversion, a re-identification, God wants to introduce us to ourselves… the real self. Not the self who has been quieted and muted by life's struggles and circumstances. No longer do we have a license to hide behind what was done to us.

Jacob's struggle recounts that he wrestled; wrestling implies a power struggle. Webster's Dictionary defines wrestle as:

"Take part in a fight, either as sport or in earnest, that involves grappling with one's opponent and trying to throw or force them to the ground."

Today the fight is on men … we are fighting for our position; to get back into position, a position that was authorized for us by God before the foundation of the world. Who is your opponent, men – you are your opponent. Not what people labeled you, not what people said about you, not your circumstance or situations. Your opponent is your inner voice, the voice that tells you, you aren't good enough, smart enough, strong enough! I come as the referee to do a count down. If you're familiar with wrestling, you know that when an opponent has been wrestled down to the mat, the referee comes and counts down to ensure that the opponent has genuinely been taken down, defeated! Before the referee can announce a winner, the opponent must truly be out for the count!

Today I pronounce your opponent, your negative self-talk, the information you have internalized and made part of your identity is cancelled. I come to announce your opponent IS DOWN FOR THE COUNT!! As with Jacob when his name was changed from Supplanter; *trickster, deceiver* to Israel; *one who has power with*

God. As we learn in Genesis 32:24-28

Afterwards, Jacob went back and spent the rest of the night alone.

A man came and fought with Jacob until just before daybreak. When the man saw that he could not win, he struck Jacob on the hip and threw it out of joint. They kept on wrestling until the man said, "Let go of me! It's almost daylight."

"You can't go until you bless me," Jacob replied.

Then the man asked, "What is your name?"

"Jacob," he answered.

The man said, "Your name will no longer be Jacob. You have wrestled with God and with men, and you have won. That's why your name will be Israel."

Men, a name change is necessary. I want you to understand the significance of Jacob's name change. A change in name is a change in God's description of you! This usually meant that God was changing your circumstance or some part of your life to fulfill His ultimate plan for you. Jacob's name was changed to Israel because of his divine encounter with God.

Allow me to examine a little deeper the significance of Jacob's name being changed to Israel. How can you apply it to yourself, men?

Firstly, Israel as a name represented a _Memorial._ Whenever his new name was mentioned, it was a reminder of what God had done for him. God gave Jacob a new birth, a new start, new identity. Men, today, God is giving us a new start, a new identity. In this new start, God is saying to you He wants you to preserve this moment and begin living from this place of newness and no more silence!

Secondly, Israel as a name was as an _Answer to Jacob's Prayer_.

Jacob prayed and told God, "*I won't let you go until you bless me.*" When God touched Jacob, he changed him, he changed his identity, he changed his character, He even changed his walk. My brothers, I've been sent to tell you everything about you is changing! No longer will you live in the defeat of your past and the curse of your failures. God is giving you new dreams, a new vision, and a new walk. One's walk from a biblical perspective often deals with a person's mode of conduct or behavior. In fact, the infinitive Greek means "to walk," and translated in Hebrew, it means "a way to live." Men, welcome to your new way of living!

Thirdly, Jacob's name change was the *Assurance of Victory* from God. Prior to the encounter, Jacob lived in a place of fear, fear of meeting his brother, fear of retribution for his past. But when Jacob prevailed with God, God would, in turn, cause him to prevail in life. Prevail – *"to prove more powerful than opposing forces; be victorious."* Men, your encounter with God, as you read this book, is to inform you, your opponent is dead, no more silence, and your victory is sure, PREVAIL! Romans 8:37:

> **Nay, in all these things we are more than conquerors through him that loved us.**

Fourthly, the name Israel is another means by which Jacob entered into a *Divine Covenant*. Israel is a name from God, while Jacob is a name that came from men based on his circumstances. Men, God, in this next season of your life, is naming you! He is covenanting with you, going into agreement with you and signing it with His blood. You will no longer be imprisoned by circumstances beyond your control, by your weakness, fragilities, and liabilities. My brother, you are who God says you are, the head and not the tail. Deuteronomy 28:13:

> **"And the Lord shall make thee the head, and not the tail; and thou shalt be above only, and thou shalt not be beneath;"**

Jacob was not born a trickster, deceiver. He became what he was called every day. It was his father who named him. But aren't you glad that *the word of man* **can be changed** by *the word of God*! As I think further about Jacob's challenge with silence, specifically the silence of identity. What in him made him acquiesce to the labels his father called him. To accept what people said about him, to the degree the Bible records, he fought to keep the wrong identity? Could his behavior be a result of what he saw his father do, a generational curse perhaps? As the saying goes, "some things are caught, not taught." Is there a case in the Bible where Isaac, Jacob's father was silent, wasn't present, or participatory in his life? I will answer that in a moment but before I do, let's explain what a generational curse is.

In the book of Exodus, we find an intriguing verse where God sternly warns that family sins can be passed down from one generation to the next. These are more commonly referred to as Generational curses. Exodus 20:4-5 NASV

"You shall not make for yourself an idol, or any likeness of what is in heaven above or on the earth beneath or in the water under the earth. You shall not worship them or serve them; for I, the Lord your God, am a jealous God, visiting the iniquity of the fathers on the children, on the third and fourth generations of those who hate me."

It was a warning God repeated several times in other passages of scripture. But here in Exodus, God admonishes Moses that the sins of the parents are passed down to children. It is as simple as your children being born with developing hypertension or a wide nose; it's hereditary.

In the Exodus passage, we can draw out several principles on generational curses that help us to understand the concept better.

"Visiting" the iniquity

The first principle is that iniquity will be "visited" upon the children. The Theological Wordbook of the Old Testament, defines the word **visit** as *"to exercise oversight over a subordinate, either in the form of inspecting or in taking action to cause a considerable change in the circumstances of the subordinate either for the better or for the worse."*

The implication is that the parent's iniquity has the right to influence the children. This does not mean that the children will automatically bend to this pressure, but it does suggest that temptations will be positioned to entice children to follow in the footsteps of their parents.

Iniquity vs. sin

The second principle we see mentioned in Exodus 20 is that it was "iniquity" that was visited upon the heirs. You may be asking the question, what is the difference between iniquity and sin? In our passage, the word **sin** is *"awon"* in Hebrew and refers to the character behind an action. Basically, iniquity can be defined as *a sin stronghold and a stronghold is **a mindset** and a mindset **materializes in addictions**.*

In Exodus, what God is warning Israel of is to turn away from their sin so that their iniquity (*sin stronghold*) would not become a stumbling block to them and their generations.

Third & Fourth Generations

Finally, we see that the ***sin stronghold*** can be passed on to the third and fourth generations. What is the depth of a generation? *A generation is twenty-five years,* and from what Exodus 20 admonishes, if Israel is not mindful of their **sin strongholds, sin addictions,** they could extend to *seventy-five* to *one hundred year*s. What does this mean? As many as three centuries of generational curses could prevail.

Now that you understand generational curses, we have a better understanding of Jacob's behavior. Could it be that Jacob was comfortable with silence because he learned it from his father Isaac and Isaac learned it from his father Abraham? The Bible records a silence that both Abraham and Isaac participated in when it came to their wives … their silence was in the form of a lie. They lied about their identity!

In Genesis 12:10-20, Abraham told Sarah to tell King Pharaoh that he was her brother, not her husband. Eight chapters later in Genesis 20:1-18, we find Abraham doing the same thing again with King Abimelech. Six chapters later in Genesis 26:7-11, Isaac is on the scene married to Rebekah. We see him perpetuating the same act, telling his wife to say to King Abimelech that he is her brother and not her husband.

I make a note of this behavior because, again, to the point made earlier, could we see a generational curse at work, passed down to Jacob. I can attest, my father's silence was generational. My grandfather (my father's father), as great as he was in giving my siblings and I anything we wanted materially, he was a silent man. He didn't do a lot of talking, and we would often observe my grandmother overtalking him. My grandfather's response would be, he would go silent. He, like my father, was a man of few words and docile. However, when he drank, he was a different man. There is a quote that says, "a drunk mind speaks a sober heart." This quote expresses the idea when a person is drunk, they lose all inhibitions and allow themselves to verbalize their true thoughts and feelings. I've seen it first-hand.

I recall times when my siblings and I would go spend the weekend with my grandparents, and if my grandfather and grandmother drank, which they both frequently did, my siblings and I could expect to see and hear a verbal fight. We would often joke about it and say it was like going to a boxing match, seeing them go back and forth at each other. If my grandfather drank, he would come back at her verbally, but if he did not drink, he would go sit in the living room in front of the television and say nothing.

For those of you reading this book, could one of the reasons for your silence be a result of what you saw as little boys from your father, and what your father saw from his father? Yes, I have often heard it said, *"it was just the culture back then. Men didn't talk much."* There is truth to that premise, and later in the book, we will hear stories from men and women corroborating this truth as experienced in their homes during their formative years.

However, when we talk about culture, who determines culture? People! Men have you been silent because of what model you saw your father portray growing up. Your mother did all the talking, not just because she was a woman, but because your father was silent. Was your father silent when it came to the affairs of the home, silent concerning finances, silent or non-participatory when it came to raising you and your siblings? Did you experience the voice of your father regularly or was it just in a dire situation when your mother needed a more authoritative voice than her own?

It is these male models that shape us, mold us and form our perception of the world, how to engage and interact with one another in various spheres of life; relationships, communities, and society.

Just as children inherit their parents' physical characteristics, the same principle is at work in the spiritual realm.

As God wrestled with Jacob to break the curse that identified him and held him hostage to the sins of his fathers, so the curse is broken today over you, my brother. You have power to speak, freedom to be, and renewed strength to walk in the destiny you were created to fulfill!

~ Questions For Reflection ~

1. What labels have been spoken over you?
2. What generational curses have you accepted as your fate?
3. Will you commit to wrestle until you are free?
4. Who do you think you are destined to be?

Chapter Three

THE POWER OF YOUR VOICE

$$Chapter\ Three$$

THE POWER OF YOUR VOICE

"Our voice is what communicates us to the world."

At all levels, and at all times, it is without a doubt the first instrument we use to communicate to the world who we are and our needs. We express this through the vehicle of our voice. Our voice expresses our deepest needs, feelings, and thoughts. Roy Hart, a pioneer in the exploration of the voice said, "The voice is the muscle of the soul." The voice is our most powerful instrument and has the greatest capacity to generate energy change and stimulate mental processes.

In preparing to write this book, I wanted to get the perspective of both males and females on the power of the voice and specifically get an idea of when growing up whose voice was the loudest, most prominent, and why.

I handpicked a panel of individuals to interview separately concerning the power of the male voice(s) in their lives. Now before we hear from these men and women, I want to present a hypnosis for your consideration.

What Shapes Your Voice

Romans 10:17-19 So then faith cometh by hearing, and hearing by the word of God. But I say, have they not heard? Yes verily, their sound went into all the earth, and their words unto the ends of the world.

Proverbs 18:21Death and life are in the power of the tongue: and they that love it shall eat the fruit thereof.

How is your voice shaped? Meaning what is it that influences the way you talk... ultimately, what influences the way you think will shape your voice? Is it your circumstances? Is it the words you hear often? Is it the people who speak those words? What shapes your voice? Remember, your life follows your words!

A baby's voice is shaped by the parent's voice. It is scientifically proven that when a baby hears his/her parents voice, the babe responds in a certain way in their brain. The amazing aspect of this is that it can happen when the baby is in the mother's womb before the baby is born.

How do you think the baby learns words – it's through the voice or words of the parent initially – whatever the baby hears, the baby learns to repeat. The baby hears the parents say, "momma and daddy," and eventually, the baby will repeat what he/she heard.

This is also the principle of creation we see in Genesis 1:1-3

In the beginning God created the heaven and the earth. And the earth was without form, and void; and darkness was upon the face of the deep. And the Spirit of God moved upon the face of the waters. And God said, Let there be light: and there was light.

Everything that God created in the universe was shaped by His word. God shapes the created order by his voice. Our world and everything in it had to be spoken into existence. And understanding this, God created mankind in His image and likeness to do the same thing. Genesis 2:7 tells us

"And the Lord God formed man of the dust of the ground and

breathed into his nostrils the breath of life; and man became a living soul."

Man Is a Speaking Spirit

Gen 2:7 reads, *"and man became a living soul."* There is an interpretation that is more precise… A more accurate interpretation. The verse actually says, ***"and man became a speaking spirit."*** God created man in His own image with the capacity to speak and communicate. Man was made a speaking spirit and given dominion. The power of speech was a major distinguishing factor between man and all of God's other creation. It is important to understand we were created speaking spirits, and our words create or world.

Let's get back to the interviews. As stated, I wanted to get various perspectives on the influence the male voice had in the lives of other people, specifically in their formative years. The group of men and women selected were asked to share their personal stories of how their father or a male voices or lack thereof impacted them.

The questions I asked the male interviewees:

1. Whose voice was the strongest in your formative years and why do you think that is?
2. What did you see displayed by your father or the predominant male in your home – was his voice strong and definitive?
3. If he was absent, how did that affect your perspective of men?
4. How does a male's voice or lack thereof affect society, community, and relationships?
5. Where did you learn the value/power of your voice?
6. Is there a male voice currently in your life making an impact?

The questions I asked the female interviewees:

1. Whose voice was the strongest in your formative years and why do you think that is?
2. What did you see displayed by your father or the predominant male in your home – was his voice strong and definitive?
3. If he was absent, how did that affect your perspective of men?
4. How does a male's voice or lack thereof affect society, community, and relationships?
5. Is there a distinction for you in the power of the male voice compared to the female voice and how?
6. Do you respect the male voice and why?

After we share the interviewees' stories, I will summarize my observations further to identify the magnitude of the male silence issue and hopefully glean possible remedies. I ask as you read the stories, prepare your hearts to learn, receive and consider if changes need to be made not only in how you define the issue but how or if you've contributed to the eradication of the male voice.

One other request – as you're reading the stories, ask yourself, who was the strongest voice in your home or community during your formative years, and what impact did it have on your perspective of the male voice and its power or lack thereof.

A brief demographic of the panel of interviewees. There were eleven people interviewed: five men, six women. They represented four different generations, the Silent Generation (born 1928–1945), the Baby Boomers (born 1946–1964), Generation X (born 1965–1980) and the Millennials (born 1981–1995).

The interviewees were raised in various locations throughout the United States. Some grew up in homes with only one parent present and some with both parents present. I intentionally selected people of varied generations to ascertain if the power of the male voice and his presence differed from generation to generation. Lastly, all the participants in my research were professing Christians whose worldview is influenced by the Bible.

THE MEN INTERVIEWED

My first male interviewee was RP. He shared his dad's voice (as he affectionately called him) was the strongest voice in his formative years. He explained that from his birth until the present age of 41, his dad's voice was the strongest voice in their home. RP told me that even after he moved out on his own, he and his dad spoke daily, and those conversations consisted of his dad providing wisdom, counsel, instructions, and rebuke when necessary. RP said, but his dad always encouraged and affirmed him. He noted that what he saw his dad display for him and his brother was what his dad learned and saw displayed from his father, RP's grandfather.

RP's dad was 20 years old when his father died, leaving him only a short time with his father. But with that short time, his dad learned what he needed to know to raise his family and lovingly take care of them. RP emphasized his dad's voice was the guiding force in his life growing up and as an adult.

RP said that having a strong male voice in his life helped him identify his voice. His dad used his life experiences, the things he did right as well as what he did wrong to help shape him into who he is today. RP stated when he was a little younger, his dad would give him "life lesson nuggets," and RP would think it didn't pertain to him because those situations hadn't happened. RP later found out at 41, a lot of what his dad told him could happen did happen. His father taught him the basic dos and don'ts; how to carry himself in public, the decorum of a minister, and the behavior of a respectful man.

RP advised it was those lessons that kept him throughout the years. His dad used himself and his life as a template for RP and his brother. The mistakes he made and the things he wished he would have done better. RP's dad told him, "I want you to do better and be better than I was and not make the same mistakes I made if you don't have to."

RP recalled how transparent his dad was in a lot of areas. In areas where he struggled or fell short as a husband, a father, a brother, and a son. His father was very active in church and demonstrated to RP and his brother how to love God.

RP said he believed the effect male silence has on society is seen in our world every day. Young men really don't have any guidance or direction. They have no clue who they are. RP said he felt that male silence hurts our younger generation, especially young men because it causes them to seek out their identity in evanescent ways, such as drugs, alcohol, gangs, and women.

RP felt if there were more consistent and a more stable male presence in the homes and communities where young boys were mentored, it would make a difference in our communities. RP elaborated the two newest generations; millennials and generation x, unfortunately, have no clue of their identity or power of the male voice.

I asked RP how did he learn the power of his voice? It was his dad who helped him, and throughout his journey, there were other great men of God that crossed his path and assisted. He said, "they help to identify certain parts of my identity." RP described them as echoes of his voice. He had pastors, mentors and colleagues who assisted in the process of identifying and honing his voice. RP said he struggled with figuring out the purpose of his voice and for many years fought allowing the opinions of others to define or drown out his authentic voice.

As we were about to close, I asked RP did he believe in the power of his own voice? He said he did believe that his voice made an impact, that it has left an imprint on the people he's encountered.

Over the past year, he has begun to ask God to help him speak up more. RP confessed that sometimes he could be a little timid and shy. As we prepared to close the interview, RP began to reminiscence on the times he's spoken up or ministered to someone and the persons often confirmed what he spoke, provided them guidance, and assistances. RP said this helped him see that if his voice empowered and affirmed one person, he has made an impact.

MP was another male I interviewed. He shared that his mother's voice was the strongest in his formative years because his father was absent, not physically absent, but absent emotionally and verbally. Although his father had a presence, it didn't equate to him being present. He shared that his father provided for the family financially but wasn't emotionally or verbally nurturing. MP resolved that his father's own issues seemed to prevent him from talking and being present for him and his siblings.

MP said his father was a silent voice in the home. He didn't offer a lot of input regarding how they were reared, what they wore, what their vocations would be, no contribution. MP elaborated that his father did not speak into his identity, and neither was he a positive influence. When he spoke the most, it was under the influence of alcohol or when flirting with women.

I asked MP how does the male voice or lack of the male voice affect society? He shared that he believes it negatively impacts society because when men have no voice, they have no identity and tend to wander aimlessly in society without direction or purpose. He stated in Biblical times, it was his understanding that the fathers were responsible for speaking into the lives of their children. By naming them, they were declaring their future and destiny. If this practice was true back then, it would reason that it still holds true today. MP believes that if fathers are not speaking into their children, identifying them, someone or something else will, possibly that being a corrupt society. Children may have their mothers and peers to influence them, but if the fathers aren't speaking into them, this keeps children in a constant search for identity.

MP elaborated this was the case with him, that his father never spoke into his identity, and therefore, he struggled with his identity.

I asked MP did this mean that he grew up asking the question, who was he? He stated yes and that this caused him to not understand the power of his voice. When the father doesn't use his voice, the son learns by example and doesn't either. MP further explained that at 50 something years of age, he's just now learning his identity and the power of his voice. For a long period of time, MP stated he tried to find validation from others, hoping someone would tell him who he was. He thought acquiring things, sleeping with multiple women, enrolling in the military would help him find his voice and it didn't.

I asked MP what was the panacea for him in finding his identity? Transparent as possible, he said, doing a self-inventory, and talking to God in prayer and ask Him what his purpose, what was he created for? MP said he didn't know what he liked really. As MP paused to speak his next phrase, he said in a low voice almost regretfully, "if only my father would have spoken into me." He didn't, and because he didn't, it has taken me all these years to begin the process of knowing myself." I allowed quietness for a moment to give MP a moment to breathe and process his thoughts. I then asked MP if he thought his father's behavior was generational, something passed down? He said yes. He believed his grandfather never told his father who he was; therefore, his father didn't know how to tell him who he was. His father couldn't give him what he had never been given himself.

As I prepared to close the interview with MP, who happens to be a father, husband, minister, and leader of a men's group, I asked him if there were male voices currently speaking into him and making an impact? He said ironically, his pastor, who was also his brother, was making an impact, and he listens to the voice of God. MP, with optimism said, "God will be a father to the fatherless."

MP said with the help of God, his pastor and the group of men he has brotherhood with are helping him to identify unchartered territories within himself that he didn't know existed. He's realizing there are reservoirs inside of him untapped and ready to be released.

My next interviewee was MS, a man with a lot of wisdom and life experiences. He explained that in his formative years, his father's voice was the most prominent one. His father set the tone for the home and the house itself. He established how things were to operate in the house, how he and his siblings were to act and behave. MS said his dad named him and his siblings to ensure the legacy of the family name was maintained.

I asked MS if his father was a very vocal person or more demonstrative in his approach? MS said, a bit of both. He was demonstrative and vocal. It depended on the situation. MS stated sometimes we don't understand silence doesn't always mean weakness. He knows that now but growing up, at one point, he thought his father was weak because he was silent. But he realized that his dad was stronger in his silence than he was vocally. His dad knew when to speak and when to give silence a voice.

MS intrigued me with this last statement, so I asked him a question, not on my list. Why did he equate silence with weakness? MS said he learned this from his mother. She had a more domineering personality than my dad. MS explained his dad was passive at times because of his upbringing. He grew up without a father and around domineering women. MS said his mom would speak the most and make certain decisions in the home. His dad would sit silently, and if things went awry, his dad would just continue in silence. But his mother would know dad was not in approval of what was going on. MS saw his dad's silence at certain times as his special powers. MS quoted a scripture that he would later relate to his dad's quiet behavior during those awry times - Isaiah 30:15 (*the later portion*):

"...in quietness and in confidence shall be your strength..."

MS explained that although his dad wasn't the most vocal person, his dad's voice was the strongest voice in the home. MS explained that he felt the lack of the male voice negatively affected society, that it gives credence to the fact that men do go unnoticed and are misunderstood. When the male voice is not heard or speaking, society tends to think that the male is not around intentionally and therefore not a part of society.

Secondly, MS said, when you look at the stance of a man, especially black men, there aren't a lot of us in professional, prominent places. So, the question becomes, who's speaking truth to our people, our young boys, and girls? Who's telling them the ins and outs and how to act or react in certain situations? If the male voice isn't doing it, it leaves to reason; society is telling them the black male voice doesn't matter.

As I prepared to close my conversation with MS, I asked him how did he learn the power of his voice? He said he learned it, one, as stated earlier from his father. But additionally, he learned it from some of the teachers that helped mold him. MS described himself as a kind of passive man like his father was. His teachers recognized he needed to be able to speak, to verbalize his thoughts. Although he could write his thoughts, he was too shy and would not speak, much less read his writings aloud. So his teachers enrolled him in different speaking competitions that forced him to learn to articulate his thoughts.

MS recalled one eighth-grade math teacher saying to him one day, "shut your black mouth." MS said when the teacher said that, he asked her, why did you say that to him? The teacher said, "because you need to learn that there are times to speak and times to be silent, and you might miss out on something you might need to know." MS said the teacher explained the importance of learning the art of listening before speaking.

I asked MS did hearing what the teacher said immobilize him or did it help him develop listening skills and learn his audience. Or did the statement stifle his voice?

MS said it did not stifle his voice because later, when he got out of the teachers' class and thought about what she said, he realized the teacher was trying to help him. The teacher had grown up between the 30s–50s and racism was heightened. The teacher saw what could happen to black men who talked a lot. The teacher even told MS that if he continued to talk a lot, "the white man was going to get him." MS said although he wasn't afraid, it did make him think. He realized that learning to listen would be key to his success, particularly since he attended a predominantly white college. This lesson from the teacher would prove to be instrumental in helping him successfully complete college during a very racist time.

Intrigued, I asked MS what did the teacher mean "If you keep talking, the white man is going to get you?" MS said the teacher explained that if he continued talking and not listening, the white man would ultimately outthink, out-educate, outsmart, and take the good jobs from him. That if he didn't take the time to listen, watch, and understand his environment, it would be to his detriment.

As I presented my last question to MS, I acknowledged his experience as a ministry leader, astute attorney, and expert in his field. I celebrated him being an author and currently working on his PhD. But I needed to know, with all he's accomplished, was the male voice important to him?

MS thoughtfully said the question was an all-consuming one. He explained when he thought about his current age that the power of the male voice is still important and key primarily because there is a generation behind him that does not know what to speak, how to speak, or how to address the issues of our current world. Issues that revolve around the black family, the church, male and female relationships, much less how to build relationships. MS said at his current age, he now knows what to say, how to say it, and the proper words to use. He said what he's learned over the years are golden nuggets that must be passed down to generations behind him. MS stated - what he does today with his voice will impact generations coming behind him.

I asked MS to further explain. He said the importance of the male voice is that we must be able to use our voice to awaken consciousness. Understanding that our voice does not have to always be loud or with words, but actions are also key. That actions directly, and indirectly affect the world around us. MS said he wants his voice to be a positive one that influences and effectuate change.

My next interviewee was AD, a millennial with a surprisingly different perspective on the male voice. AD was raised by his grandfather, someone from the Greatest generation era (it's labeled), born between 1901 – 1927. His grandfather was the prominent voice in his home even though his voice was quiet, and he didn't talk a lot. His presence was very strong in the home. His grandfather made sure everything in and around the house was taken care of.

AD said his grandfather was the type of provider that provided not only materially but also emotionally. However, his grandfather wasn't an emotionally affectionate person. I asked AD to explain. He said his grandfather was not verbally affirming, he was born in 1918, and men from that era did not normally encourage with words. They were taught to provide and protect the family, and that is how they showed their love.

AD said what he saw his grandfather display was financial

stewardship. He paid the bills, provided for the upkeep of the house, and ensured everyone had clothes to wear and protected the family. But grandfather did not talk a lot. He did more listening than talking. With this backdrop, I asked AD in watching his grandfather model what a man looked and acted like, and with his birth father not being present in his life, what did he learn about the importance of the male voice or its absences in the community.

AD stated he feels our communities are negatively affected when there is no male voice. AD gave this analogy. He said, "the black man specifically is the white man of the black community," meaning the black man is the pillar of the community. He is the one that everything and everybody looks to. Everything falls on his shoulders, and if he fails, the community fails. AD noted the incarceration of black men, black-on-black crime, blacks killing blacks exemplifies this failure in our society. When the man has no voice, no presence, it affects the entire community negatively.

AD being my youngest interviewee, I asked if he knew the power of his own voice. Had anyone ever told him? His answer was honest yet insightful. He first said, let me think about it, and then he explained that his interpretation of having a voice is not always audible. He said personally he's not a big talker, but his voice is what he demonstrates every day to others. His voice is heard in how he treats people, his actions, and how he conducts himself in the community. He defines his voice by his actions.

I thought, wow! This young man gets it. The voice is not limited to only sound, but also what we show people. There is a saying that holds true – "actions speak louder than words." I shared with AD that he was right. A voice is not always necessarily audible, but that it does represent identity, authority, and the core of who a person is. I asked AD where did he learn the power of his voice or was he still learning? He said he was still learning and that he didn't think that was something taught in our community. He said he was still becoming more confident as he matures and realizing what he brings to the world.

In closing out our interview, I asked AD, were there any male voices speaking into him, making a deposit into his identity? AD said there were two men he could count on to speak into him. I asked, how does their voice impact your life?

AD said they helped him to become more focused on his goals and spiritually grounded. AD closed out our conversation, saying, "it's like what I tell my students, focus on what you need to focus on, and all the other stuff will come."

I talked with LB, another established professional male whose perspective was quite refreshing. LB explained his dad's voice was the most predominant one in the home during his formative years. Although his mom and dad didn't subscribe to the traditional gender roles in the home, it was always clear his dad was the head of the household, but this did not diminish the role of his mom.

LB said his dad always made sure he and his brothers knew anything their mom said, Dad backed her up 100%. His mom also made sure the boys knew there was a male presence in the home. What was most respectful of both parents LB said was they never allowed he and his brothers to pit one parent against the other. If one parent established a rule, the other parent supported the rule. LB said his dad had dominance in the house, but it was shared between both parents.

LB said when his mom got sick, dad, as head of the house, postured himself to reassure them there was no need to worry about finances. He would take care of the household even if it meant getting a second job. His dad was also a strong spiritual role model who demonstrated the importance of having a relationship with Christ and attending church no matter what. LB and his brothers understood if dad could work two jobs and go to church every Sunday, so could they.

LB further explained that his dad wasn't one of those men giving the impression that having three boys, it wasn't okay for men to show love. His dad made sure that he showed them love all the time, verbally and physically. LB said his dad would hug and kiss them even at his strong towering stature of 6'6". His dad was mild-tempered and not afraid to be vulnerable.

LB described that his dad was very affectionate and would always tell people how much he loved his boys. He loved to laugh and joke but also made sure they understood the importance of respecting their elders and others. LB said you could feel the affection from my dad while at the same time experiencing his power and strength.

I thought what a paradox and rarity in many black homes, a seemingly well-balanced man strong in his identity. LB said it was nothing unusual for them to experience affirmation verbally and physically.

I asked LB did he think the absence of the male voice negatively affected our communities? He stated, it does and how unfortunate when men don't have guidance, or a model of what manhood looks like. He shared that he has male friends who were raised by their mothers only, and they had to figure out what it meant to be a man on their own. And if the mother had a couple of boyfriends coming in and out of the house this often created a situation for them as young boys to seek identity. LB's friends shared, they began to feel like it was their responsibility to be the man of the house. This would manifest when they as young boys would start being rebellious towards their mothers and disrespectful toward the men in their mother's life.

LB finalized his thought by saying these young boys grew up to be men in search of their identity and being vulnerable, they misinterpret what a man is. They start conjuring up ideals of what a man is through what they saw on television. LB said there are so many men suffering in silence, depression, and anxiety because of the absence of the male voice.

I asked LB at what point did he learn the power of his voice? He said in his early 20s when he realized he needed to do some things differently. His Dad told him and his brothers, when they turned 18, they had to do one of three things; go to college, go to work, or go into the military. He had to figure it out for himself, and it was at that point, he realized his own voice and started speaking what he wanted to do and be into existence.

My last question to LB was how important is the male voice to him? Being an established doctor, in a career he's been in over a decade; consider the voice of wisdom to many of his colleagues and senior leadership, is the male voice important? LB said, the male voice is absolutely important. But also, he feels some of the casualties of the male voice being silenced is that silence has causes men and society to suffer in so many ways. Because of the silence, men don't get a chance to express who they really are and what they desire. This leads to perpetual procrastination and the inability to believe that you can be more or do more than what you currently see or experience. LB said, unfortunately, the plight of where you are can easily keep you in the place of complacency. And the complacency turns into silence which causes a man to stop dreaming. LB shared at one point, he had to decide that he no longer was going to be silent because God had given him the ability to speak.

Through exposure, he learned to unmute himself and not allow anyone to quiet his voice any longer, including his own fears. No longer would the fear of what someone said or thought about him paralyze him. He was comfortable in his own skin, comfortable with his own voice, and felt he had something to say and others could benefit from his voice.

Before I share the women's interviews, I would like to summarize what I believe the men shared concerning what they needed from their fathers. Matthew 3:16-17 describes it best men need: ***affirmation***, ***acceptance***, ***adoration,*** and ***approval***.

- ***Affirmation – emotional support, encouragement, stating one's position.***
  - ⇒ This is what the Father did with Jesus at his Baptism, He provided the emotional support by stating to the world who he was, HIS SON. As men, we need the father's voice to state who we are, sons. This is the power of the father's voice.
- ***Acceptance – the action of consenting or receiving what has been offered.***
  - ⇒ The Father consented or received who Jesus was, what he offered. His acceptance showed Jesus as HIS SON. Jesus had not yet performed one miracle or died on one cross. His Father received him as he was. Every man needs to be received by his father not because of what he does but because he is a son. When he is not accepted, he experiences rejection which causes him to wander like Cain; feeling cursed, he hides or wears a mask.
- ***Adoration – deep love and respect.***
  - ⇒ God had no problem telling the world that he adored his son, Jesus. As a beloved son, Jesus knew that his father was crazy about him, and he didn't care who knew it. Men need Fathers that will express unceasing love towards them. Love that says you are my treasure and delight. Men yearn for this Father love; it heals every broken place in their soul.

- *Approval – officially agree or accept as satisfactory.*
    - ⇒ The Father at Jesus' Baptism announced His approval when He said, "in whom I'm well pleased." He was telling everyone He officially agrees or validates HIS SON. Men long for their fathers to tell them they are good at something. There is no other compliment greater than a father to his son. Why do you think men seek validation in all the wrong places? Because they are attempting to fill what I call the father void.

THE WOMEN INTERVIEWED

My first female interviewee was AI. She shared that the strongest voice in her home during her formative years was her mom because she was stern and always talking. Ms. AI described her father as not being boisterous but one who demonstrated love by his actions. She said her father taught her how men should treat a lady, what a gentleman looked like.

AI recalled although her father didn't speak a lot, his actions spoke loudly. What he demonstrated by his actions taught her valuable lessons. When he did talk, there was substance and you wanted to listen. I asked AI did she think the male voice or lack of the male voice affected society negatively? She stated yes because men have been created to operate like God and their simple presence can affect an environment. I asked Ms. AI how she would define presence. Is it the same thing as being present? She said no; presence doesn't always mean engagement. Engagement is more important than presence. AI said when it comes to the male voice being silent or absent from society, relationships, and the community, it gives women a bad rap because when the man is silent, the woman must speak up.

MS AI further stated that to have better jobs, better neighbors, better communities, and better relationships, it has to start with us.

Silence of the Lad, Why Men Stop Talking

We all must adopt a kingdom mindset. I asked Ms. AI if she respected the male voice. She said yes and that women need to learn to be submissive again. Being submissive is not a negative thing, but have been viewed negatively. She made the point that people are submissive to their jobs. If they work a 9:00 to 5:00 they are required to be there on time and submit to a boss. That is submission.

I asked AI, in her own personal relationships had she experienced a man going silent on her, and if so, how did she interpret his silence, and how did it impact her? Ms. AI first stated that there is an adage that says a happy wife, a happy life. She confessed that she didn't exactly buy into the philosophy, and the reason was that when you have a silent man, often times, he has inverted his feelings. How can you have a happy life if your man is not happy and silent, it's selfish. When he can't come home and find peace, he goes silent. When he can't express his emotions, he goes silent.

Ms. AI said she often believes, when men are quiet, it's because they are made to be quiet through the circumstances they experience. She said although she doesn't want a man who is a whiner crying all the time, she does desire a man who knows how to express himself and take his rightful place as head of the home. Ms. AI said she believes a man can be strong and silent. But also, women must present themselves as someone the men can talk to, trust, and confide in. Women must learn to ask the right questions and not be so selfish and self-centered.

My next interview was with Ms. BP, a mother, minister, and professional woman. She advised that during her formative years she didn't have a male figure in her life to respect his voice. Her stepfather didn't have a voice. He wasn't one to speak his opinion. I probed BP to find out what did she mean by "he didn't have a voice?"

She said he did not express himself verbally. He was silent. He was silent in the house and felt his job was to go to work, bring the money home and take care of the household. BP further explained her stepfather didn't really have many conversations with her. He never inquired about her day at school or anything. Her mom was a stay-at-home mom, and they didn't want for anything financially, but her stepfather was silent. Ms. BP said they didn't even have conversations at the dining table during various meals.

I inquired of Ms. BP, how did her stepfather's silence affect her impression of men and the power of their voice? Ms. BP advised because he didn't display a strong voice, she never thought about the power of a man's voice. However, it did impact how she chose men when dating - she didn't know what to look for in a man. She explained her stepfather never sat down to explain to her what a good man was or otherwise. In hindsight, Ms. BP saw her stepfather as being unprotective of her. Although he didn't want me talking to boys, he never told me why. So as she matured, she would often choose the wrong man to date.

I asked Ms. BP how does the male voice, or the lack of the male voice affect society, relationships, and the community as a whole? Ms. BP explained that in her experience, even having three boys of her own, she saw them get quiet because of the lack of male influence. They didn't know how to communicate well, they were angry, and I didn't know what to do. Ms. BP said so, she went to the church, got the boys involved with activities at church, and asked her pastor to mentor them. But that didn't work because they were 15 and 16 years old, needing their father, and no other male could talk to them, they didn't have an initial respect for the male voice.

Ms. BP further stated, when men have no voice in our culture, it is viewed as weakness. They can't express themselves emotionally, so they find an outlet that often is criminal activity, but it's actually a cry for help and no one sees that. Society often looks at this behavior as another negative indecent black men perpetuate, not realizing that black men need someone to talk to, specifically they need to speak with other men.

Ms. BP said another thing she noticed in the silence of the male voice, men don't seek professional help, specifically in the black community. Counseling is considered taboo. Ms. BP said, she believes counseling could help many men because it would give them another perspective, a possible outlet. Ms. BP said she told her boys who grew up without their father in the home, they had a heavenly father who loved them. She instilled in them the importance of going to church and getting mentored by the pastor to be strong black men.

I asked Ms. BP did that decision impact her boys positively; she said she believed it made a difference, but she wished she would have done it sooner, but because of her pride, attesting that she didn't want anyone in her business, her boys suffered. After she shared that, I thought to myself, how often have we in our community not reached out for help and assistance because of misplaced pride which ultimately negatively affects our families.

I asked Ms. BP did she think there was a distinction between the male and female voice as far as its impact. She said absolutely. The female voice did not have the same authority that a male voice did. She could tell her boys to stop doing something and they would ignore her and continue doing what she told them to stop doing. But if she threated them by saying she would call their father, the house would immediately go silent, and they would cease being defiant.

Their father could walk in the house and anything he told them to do, they would do. Their father wasn't one to discipline them with a belt, but he would discipline them by making them do chores around the house, sit-ups, push-ups, and physical exercises. He was former military and discipline involved chores and strenuous physical exertions. In his mind, that was punishment.

Ms. BP explained at the end of the day, the male voice and his presence makes a difference.

My last question to Ms. BP was did she respect the male voice? And if so, why? And if not, why? BP said she did respect the male voice and the reason was because the tone of a man's voice is different from a woman. She however, adamantly stated, the tone must be right, not yelling or screaming at her but talking to her calmly and with respect. And more importantly, if he's a man of God, she can respect him because she feels he's coming with the heart of God and will not hurt her.

Ms. BP stated a man's voice is very powerful when he speaks truth in love, not hatred, not because of an argument and trying to get back at her but speaking the truth in love. This is when she can really respect and honor the man's voice. Ms. BP said she thought the sound of a man' voice, whether in the physical or the spirit, is much different than a woman's voice.

Ms. BP said in closing, women must be careful how they speak to a man because they can cut him to the core and take his dignity and rob him of his manhood by her words. Because women are fast talkers, they can often do that. Ms. BP believes it's this behavior that contributes to a man going silent. As Ms. BP reminiscence on her experiences, she said that she grew up in a home where her stepfather couldn't out talk her mother, so he put his hands on her. Growing up in this environment created some aggression in Ms. BP that she had to learn to manage.

Ms. BP vowed to herself that she would never allow a man to put his hands on her. However, this behavior caused her to raise her sons in a manner that made them emotionally hard and shut off, which she regrets.

In talking with Ms. TP another very strong woman who has been able to climb the corporate ladder, purchase a great home and realize some of her life dreams without a husband, I asked her who was the strongest voice in her formative years. She said it would have to be a female, not a male. I asked her why did she think that was?

Ms. TP said it was based upon the dynamics of the household she grew up in. Although a part of her life, her father wasn't in the household, so that meant, of course, she spent more time with her mom, and so, therefore, her mom was the dominant voice. Ms. TP shared that her father had a very strong personality,

I asked Ms. TP, though your father was present in your life but not in the home and your mom's voice was the stronger because you grew up in the house with her, do you think that impacted your perspective or your view of men growing up?

Ms. TP advised she felt it was tainted. It colored it a bit. It colored it in that her mother ran the household. She was mother and father. She was the one in the household. Although her father was old-school and older than her mother, her father was one who believed the man is the head, the leader. In alignment with the word of God. The conflict, however, was what she witnessed day in and day out, a woman functioning as head of the household, and growing up, that created conflict within herself.

Intrigued, I asked Ms. TP how did it create conflict? Was it about relationships? Was it about respect and honor? What type of conflict did it create? She related the conflict to having to do with what the Bible taught, and being in ministry, she believed the word of God to be true. Its principles were infallible, so because she believed the word of God, what she believed and what she witnessed contradicted each other and therefore created the conflict throughout her life in various areas.

Ms. TP went on to say that she respects men and looks at them as being the head of the home according to scripture. But it wasn't what she saw growing up. Ms. TP said candidly she respects men and their role, but because of her rearing, she views it maybe a little harsher than perhaps some women. Ms. TP said, she owns her home, runs her household, pays her bills, and takes care of her business, she does what needs to be done. But if a man came into her life, she wouldn't have a problem allowing him to be the head. Ms. TP said, "if he worked every day and was a hard worker. If he did things around the house, lifted things, picked things up, move things, fix things, did those things for me that would equate to being useful in the household."

I presented my next question to Ms. TP and said, you are a successful adult woman who's in ministry, who is a leader in her own right, who has a position in which she deals with power figures every day, how does a male voice or the lack of a male voice affect our society, community, and relationships from your perspective?

Ms. TP said she believes the silence of the male voice is one of the great lacks in the community. Ms. TP said she thinks of it like building blocks. The male is the building block, the male's voice, and his presence is the building block of the community but its missing. In her mind, it's like a house of cards all tumbling down around us, on top of us, over us. Part of the problem is the lack of the male presence. Somewhere we missed the point, gotten off track as a society, specifically in the black experience.

Ms. TP said many women are of the persuasion that if a man is not making the money or the most money in the household, if he's not able to buy the big house, if he's not able to buy the expensive cars and the clothes and the jewelry and all those things, then he's not useful. When you have the socioeconomic issues of today that we've experienced, I would say within the last 40-50 years, that have caused a lot of men to take a back seat to women in the marketplace. That is a problem. When we talk about households, you have the male, the female, and the children. If they could come together that is one level of relationships, then they create the next level, which is the household and then the households come together and create the next level, which would be the neighborhoods in the community. And then the communities come together to create the society.

For some reason, men have been taken out of the equation, and therefore the foundation is no longer solid, it's shaky! Men have been removed because we feel that if he's not contributing financially, the way the woman is, or more than she is, then he's no longer useful. And a lot of that has to do with, I think the men and what they believe about themselves. They've bought into a system that defames them and sells them out.

Captivated by this conversation, I asked Ms. TP how does she personally interact with a man who knows you don't need him financially?

Ms. TP said for her, she doesn't look at man's worth based on what he can give her financially. All that stuff she doesn't focus on. But she focuses on love. Her mother teased her saying, "girl, you know that love is not going to feed you and the kids." Her mother further teased, saying, "you take that love to that Safeway and put them groceries up on that belt and tell the cashier you are paying with love." But Ms. TP says she's wired that way to believe in the power of love.

Ms.TP shared that her thoughts on the man and his influence, she doesn't need him to pay the mortgage or purchase cars and do those things, but she needs him to hang the drapes, bring the case of water in from the car, be there for her emotionally, spiritually and a sounding board. Be the place of wisdom and safety for her, to protect and profess.

As I prepared to wrap up my conversation with Ms. TP, I asked her, so when you think about the male voice in comparison to the female voice, and you understand that I'm not just talking about vocal cords or the tone of the man's voice, but about the authority the male voice represents, that God in creating Adam gave him authority in his voice to the point that Adam was charged to name the creation and even named his wife.

With this understanding, when you think about it in your own personal experiences and life story, what do you think the distinction is in a male voice compared to a female voice? What separates the two?

Ms. TP explained the male voice is the place of authority; it's a place of authority and almost a bravado. The authority that is not based on what he brings in the house or his paycheck but his authority, his God-given identity.

I asked Ms. TP if she thought she was an anomaly in the way she thought about the male. She said to some degree, but she realizes in order to build up the family, the community, and society as a whole, the man must be built up! I sat on the other end of the phone thinking WOW!

My final question to Ms. TP was, what can the male do to make his voice heard? Ms. TP said it's going to take the intervention of God, real intervention. That the condition we are in with men and his position in society has gone on so long that it's a cancer, and at some point, when cancer reaches every cell, it just gets so bad there is nothing that can be done. Ms. TP said sadly, it's almost like that, society is heading down that road but if men step up and know their worth, that their voice can effect change in families, community, and the society. If the male would begin to know his worth, that he can still be head of the household even if his paycheck doesn't match his wife.

I closed by saying to Ms. TP, this conversation was really enlightening and as you know, all this started in the Garden of Eden when what man was created to do, speak into, and give life to, he stop doing when he went silent.

Ms. TP said, and "because of that, the village is on fire, what should have been growing, starting with the family, then the community and ultimately the society is being torn down … the village is on fire."

After taking a rest from my conversation with Ms. TP, the next interview was with Ms. EP. She shared a transparent and realistic perspective with her experience as it related to the power of the male voice. Ms. EP grew up in a home where although her father wasn't present, her brother had a strong male influence on her. Her mother was a strong woman as well and outspoken, but Ms. EP desired the power and authority of a male voice, what she saw displayed by her brother.

Ms. EP explained that because she learned how to take care of herself being around her brother, she also learned how to fight like a man if necessary. If a man came around Ms. EP, he had to know the power of his voice. Ms. EP said she believes the absence of the male voice has negatively affected relationships, the community and society. She has seen it firsthand and has had to take upon herself the responsibility of playing the role of both sexes where necessary.

I asked Ms. EP how in the past did she deal with the silence of a man? She adamantly advised when men go silent because she knows how to fight for herself and get things done, she would pick up her "manhood," as she called it, and press on. The silence of a man in a relationship causes her to move on and take on the perspective that she does not really need the man. Her feelings about male silence, "if he wants to be silent, he can be silent alone, I have no need for him." Ms. EP continued to state when men are silent in the community, in relationships, and society, it is not a good thing. Life has taught her if the man chooses to go mute, he should be by himself. She closed our conversation by stating her perspective may be terrible to some, but it's been her method of survival.

Ms. PW was my next interview. She advised the strongest voice in her home growing up was her father. He was the disciplinarian and whatever he said, it was the law.

I asked her how did that affect her growing up, specifically in understanding the power of the male voice, was her father authoritative, affirming or did he engender more fear in the home? Ms. PW said he was authoritative in terms of you had to listen and pay attention to him. However, it turned into fear because of the experiences she had with her father. She recalled her father being very defensive, angry, and regretful all the time. His behavior changed throughout the years.

I probed Ms. PW to see if her father was affectionate and affirming, or was he abusive physically and verbally? Ms. PW stated, he was all the above. He could be very caring at times and abusive at other times. The abuse became a pivotal point in her relationship with her father and she began to fear him. In exchange her interaction with her father in those formative years caused her to be defensive and angry with men in her future. Because she didn't understand why her father abused her, she because defensive and non-trusting of men.

Ms. PW's response alarmed me. I asked Ms. PW, with the abuse experiences, how did this impact her perception of the power of the male voice? She said because of the abuse, she became very defensive towards men and didn't trust them anymore. Neither did she appreciate their authority over her life. She became defensive and didn't want to talk to or be in the presence of her father. After these experiences, Ms. PW began to view the male voice and men from a negative lens, a place of fear and mistrust.

Although this occurred in her formative years, she does believe as an adult, the male voice is very important to society and it's important that black women learn to respect the male voice because he is biblically the head of the home. Ms. PW continued her train of thought and said it is important that women learn how to submit and trust the men in their life. Her reply was reminiscent of what Ms. AI shared in her prior interview. Trust takes time, but it is possible to develop it. Her observation concerning the male voice was that women often diminished the power of his voice by disrespecting him and minimizing his contribution or calling him out of his name.

I asked Ms. PW if she respected the male voice, specifically after all she experienced with the abuse during her formative years. She surprisingly said yes because it was time for her to let go of her past. That she needed a strong man in her life not just for physical strength but also social and intellectual strength. Ms. PW advised she needed someone she could respect and trust his position as the man in her life.

I said to Ms. PW, realizing there was a major trauma she had experienced from the hand of the male model in her life. I paused to give Ms. PW a moment to breath and then said, Ms. PW with you having accomplished some major things in your life; you're a ministry leader, an author and entrepreneur, do you believe there is a distinction between the power of the male voice compared to the power of the female voice, and if so, what? Ms. PW asks if she could think about the question for a moment. She then said, the distinction is she believes a woman needs a man, and even though she's very successful in some areas, in other areas, she is unsuccessful and needs a man to speak into her. She feels companionship is important

As I closed the conversation with MS. PW, she shared with me that men's silence in relationships has always been an issue because she didn't know how to interpret his silence. It caused her to do one of several things, ask the man if she did something wrong, inquire if she could do anything to help make him talk, or she would become angry and kick the man to the curb. How she dealt with male silence was based on her past relationships, bad memories, and the abuse she experienced with her father and other relationships.

My final female interview was with Ms. RB. She shared at age

10 her father was killed, and therefore, her mom's voice was the predominant voice in the home. But her mother's voice didn't carry the same weight as her father's voice. She loved and was very close to her father and was with him before he passed. Ms. RB stated she was in awe of her father. Although a man short in stature, shorter than her mom, he was never abrasive, pushy, or demanding. He was a well-balanced man. Her father made an indelible imprint in her life, and when he died, for a while, she would still hear his voice in her head. I asked Ms. RB, with her father leaving her life at such an early age did that leave a male void in her life, and if so, what did she substitute his voice with?

Ms. RB shared that she looked to her siblings to take care of her, and when they didn't, which also almost caused her to almost get kidnapped by a stranger. She decided as a young girl, to depend on herself. Her voice became the dominate voice. Although she yearned for her father and would often see images of him in various places, she knew her father was no longer physically with her. She recalls seeing him sitting, waiting for her in front of her house one day and as she got closer to the house, the image disappeared.

Ms. RB said when her father was alive, he had a strong presence and spent a lot of time with her. I asked Ms. RB does she think the absence of the male voice makes a difference in the community, relationships, and society. She said yes that in God's original creation, He created man and made him in His likeness and image." She said she thinks there is a godliness in men. They were created to be the head. It is important that men lead as God created them, that from her perspective their leading makes them godly as long as they aren't dictators. Ms. RB continued stating that it is important to see men in the community and that men have certain roles in the community to help the community thrive. When they are absent, there is major impact on the community.

Ms. RB said in her own experience, although it seemed that her mom did everything, disciplined her, taught her schoolwork, spanked her when she was wrong, it did not diminish the role and voice of her father. Ms. RB said in God's original creation, He created the man and woman to be a unit and work together in harmony.

Ms. RB said, looking back at her marriage, there were certain things she wanted to be valued in her family, but there weren't a lot of harmonious communication between she and her ex-husband. Ms. RB elaborated about the challenges men and women have in relationships, men often wanting to execute their power or voice over the voice of the woman.

I asked Ms. RB if she thought there was a distinction between the powers of the female voice and the male voice? And if so, what is the distinction between the two? Ms. RB asked a qualifying question – did I mean as it should be or as it currently is? I replied, tell me as it is and how you think it should be.

Ms. RB said yes, there is a distinction, most children are raised by their mothers and because of this, the mother's voice tends to be both the voice for the father and mother. And because this was the voice of the mother, her voice was predominant. The mother often was the one who had all the responsibility of raising the children. This caused the man's voice to go mute because the woman did what she had to do to keep her family going. Ms. RB said she saw this with her mom, but when her father did speak, his voice carried with it an authority that her mom didn't have. Mothers would have to tell the children something repeatedly, but when fathers spoke, there was an authority it seemed attached to their voice.

As I prepared to close my interview with Ms. RB, I said to her, let me ask you a question. In doing these interviews and my goal in writing this book is not to fix men. I don't have a crystal ball and I can't fix anything. But the goal is to bring awareness to not only females but to men concerning the power of their voice and how society and our communities need the male voice. The goal is also to bring an awareness to women concerning why men sometimes go silent and what women can do to encourage the men to talk.

Ms. RB stated that she felt for so long, men do not get a fair chance. Women often outnumber men, eight to one, it used to be, she said. She than stated, this has been hurtful to men. Eight women saying that "a man is weak." You have eight women saying that "man is no good." You have eight women saying that "oh, he's a dog," and you have one man trying to communicate … but he can't get past or outnumber eight women. Ms. RB said - so the man's default is, "well, why am I going to talk … because if I don't say what you want me to say, you don't want to listen to me anyway." I thought to myself WOW – isn't that often the emotions of us as men – and if we aren't going to be heard, why talk.

My last question to Ms. RB, who herself was an established, professional nurse by training, pastored a large church and raised her family, who now her children were adults with families of their own. Ms. RB, when it comes to the silence of a man, how has it impacted you? She said because man was created to speak, when he doesn't speak, the world around him remains in darkness. There's a degree of darkness that exists because the man has not spoken to it. Yes, God created the world and the earth, but He told Adam to speak to the creation and begin to name it. Men must take back their rightful place on the earth and begin speaking, using their voice of authority to create.

I'm appreciative of all my interviewees. As with the men, the women shared priceless nuggets that must be considered. The women spoke to the necessity of the man's voice being:

resurrected, released, revitalized, and *received*

- ***Resurrected – brought back to life.***

⇒ The man's voice must be resurrected. Nothing dead can bring life. Like Lazarus, when Jesus spoke to his grave, He wasn't intimidated nor hindered by the smell of death. Women, you have the power to resurrect your man. Create an environment of acceptance and trust for him and reap the benefits.

- *Released – allowed or enabled to escape from confinement, set free.*

  ⇒ Typically, when something is released, there is someone granting permission. Who will give the man permission to come out of confinement, hiding, silence? Don't allow the man to pretend any longer, women he's looking for your permission to be free. Start listening to understand and not to criticize.

- *Revitalized – imbue something with new life.*

  ⇒ Today is the day of new beginnings. Women, I believe you have been equipped with what it takes to breathe new life into the man in your life. I believe this because when God created him, man, God had you in mind. You were in the man at creation. Stop fussing and start feeling – connect. To breathe life into someone, you must get mouth-to-mouth.

- *Received – to be given.*

  ⇒ The season of rejection is over. We shared one of the greatest fears of a man is rejection. He goes into hiding when he's rejected. Look at Adam. Women, what will it take to receive your man, receive his heart, receive his words, and receive his love? He may not do it exactly like you want but is he willing to do it and if so - Receive him!

Everything Has A Voice

When we look at creation, it is eye-opening to first understand that everything God created has a voice. The tree's voice is heard as the leaves blow in the wind, the river's voice sings as the waters splash against the embankment. The owl's voice is heard in the sound of the hooting. Everything that God created has a voice. So when the male loses his voice, I submit, it throws the order of creation off. Let us examine this premise a little deeper from scripture.

In the original Hebrew regarding the Creation, the ancient Jewish perception and interpretation of the events encompassing Creation and HOW God created the world as seen in the phrase "and God said."

The implication is creation occurred by the power of SPEAKING. According to the Jewish tradition, the world was created as *God spoke*, along with every single other created thing composing His Creation.

We understand the origins of this tradition as we examine the word of God and say that 'God said, as seen in the following examples:

"And God SAID, "Let there be light," and there was light." (Genesis 1:3)

"And God SAID, "Let there be an expanse in the midst of the waters, and let it separate the waters from the waters." (Genesis 1:6)

"And God SAID, "Let the waters under the heavens be gathered together into one place, and let the dry land appear." And it was so." (Genesis 1:9)

What is interesting to discover is that in the case of the light, heaven, and earth, there was another important aspect of God's voice that must be highlighted. After God spoke, He "named" identified. Purpose was given to the thing he spoke to as revealed in the following examples:

"God called the light Day, and the darkness he called Night."

"And God called the expanse Heaven"

"God called the dry land Earth, and the waters that were gathered together he called seas."

The usage of verbs that are related to speaking, such as 'said' and 'called' led to the perception that LANGUAGE played a significant role in the process of the Creation. In fact, there is an entire division of studies that deals with this subject and is called in Hebrew 'Ma'ase Bereshit' - the act of the Creation of the world.'

'Ma'ase Bereshit' is a part of ancient Jewish literature, which interpreted the Torah according to the 'fourth pillar of Jewish Bible interpretation,' which is called 'Sod' - Hebrew for 'secret' and refers to the deeper layers of God's words that are 'hidden' in the Bible and therefore requires a certain method of studying the Bible.

I share all of this because we see the principle of God "speaking creation into existence and then naming or identifying the various elements of creation. Adam was the first creation; and notice he was called to name what God didn't name. The Bible says: "And out of the ground Jehovah God formed every beast of the field, and every fowl of the air; and brought them to Adam to see what he would call them: and whatever Adam called every living creature, that was the name thereof.

And Adam gave names to all cattle, and to the fowl of the air, and to every beast of the field" (Genesis 2:19–20).

Whenever I read these verses prior, I always thought: Adam named all the animals, all the birds and all the beasts of the field. He must have known all these living things; otherwise, how would he have come up with so many names? God must have told him beforehand, right. Whatever the case, the amazing eye-opener for me is that Adam, naming God's creation, reveals a principle that God started with the man and man is charged to continue … **His voice and speech have the power to create and identify.**

For this to be significant, you must understand what it means to create. To create, as revealed in Genesis 1, is the word **bara,** "created" in Genesis 2, the word used when he creates the man is *yatsar*, meaning "fashioned," a word used in contexts such as a potter fashioning a pot from clay.

We aren't called to *bara,* create out of nothing, only God can do that. But we are called to *yatsar*, fashion things out of what is already here.

Men, it's our time to speak up again; everything we need to make what we want is on the earth, but we won't see it manifested until we speak it!

I challenge each of you reading this book, and specifically men, realize you have been given your voice to speak, to *yastar*, to create the world Jesus Christ died to give you!

YOUR VOICE HAS POWER SO

YASTAR!

~ Questions For Reflection ~

1. Take a moment and reflect on the power of your voice.
2. Do you know how to use your voice?
3. What have you created lately with your voice?
4. What are you feeding your mind that influences what your voice speaks?

Chapter Four
THE TRAUMA

Chapter Four
THE TRAUMA

"There are wounds that never show on the body that are deeper and more hurtful than anything that bleeds."

Trauma is defined as: **an emotional response to a terrible event like an accident, rape, or natural disaster. Immediately after the event, shock and denial are typical. Longer-term reactions include unpredictable emotions, flashbacks, strained relationships and even physical symptoms like headaches or nausea.**

Trauma is pertinent to my story and one of the reasons why I think I sunk deeper into the abyss of silence. Although I didn't realize I had experienced trauma, much less knew what it was. As I grew up into manhood and became exposed to various mediums of thought, new information and exposure to psychology by working in the mental health field for several years. I learned some things about the brain and how a person could experience different disorders due to trauma. Disorders such as:

Dissociative Identity Disorder (DID). *Formerly called Multiple Personality Disorder*. This is a mental health condition. Someone with DID has multiple, distinct personalities. The various identities control a person's behavior at different times. This condition can cause memory loss, delusions, or depression. DID is usually caused by past trauma.

Depersonalization/Derealization Disorder, another mental health condition. People with this condition are detached from thoughts, feelings, and body (depersonalization) and disconnected from their environment (derealization). These feelings could be caused by alarm but may not be the cause of the person being alarmed.

Borderline Personality Disorder, another mental health condition. People with this condition have difficulties managing emotions effectively. They tend to be unstable in their relationships, self-image, and emotions. People with this condition experience rapid changes in mood that could last from a few hours to a few days. They may also experience issues of identity, self-harm, impulsivity, fear of abandonment, and feelings of emptiness.

I listed those disorders because what I realized was each disorder could be triggered by trauma. Although in the religious community, we don't like to label or identify these issues in "the saints," God allowed the profession of medicine for a reason; one to help assist in diagnosing some of the maladies that mankind experience. Yes, I do believe we shouldn't label ourselves and restrict our identity to the diagnosis of the medical field, however, I do believe we can learn something from the medical field. If nothing else, how to command deliverance from these issues in prayer for the community of believers plagued by these traumas.

But that is not the point I'm making here. I shared these different disorders because of what I didn't know. As a young boy and young adult male who experienced the various traumas I did, a doctor could have diagnosed me with every one of these disorders. I truly lived in an altered reality and this was my method of coping. It was nothing for me to go into excessive mood swings, experience silent depression and suicidal ideations. To have multiple personalities, in my mind, I would be different people depending on the audience I was in. I was also good at detaching emotionally and disassociating from people.

Although I never graduated into self-cutting or self-mutilation, the trauma I'd experienced in my formative years into young adult manifested itself in my actions and behaviors. But I'm sharing this with you also because the purpose of my book is to look at what causes a little boy, an adult man, to go mute, silent? For me, it was not only the subliminal messaging I received from my father growing up, telling me I didn't have a voice, but the situations that occurred, traumas also took my voice, muted me.

Trauma caused me to go silent. I named the book silence of the lad because I was a lad, a little boy, when all this occurred.

I will chronicle for you some of the traumas I recall that stole my voice. It is funny because, thank God, I'm so healed from these things; I had to sit down and make myself remember to rehearse some of the incidents. As I write them, they no longer have a stink or cause any type of embarrassment or shame. But in those seasons of my life, they did and it was so easy to keep silent about them.

I want to stop for a moment and share a principle with you that I think is important to understand. When you meet a little boy, a young man or adult man and he appears, timid, shy, or afraid, I'm not encouraging you to diagnosis the young lad, but understand that he could have experienced some type of trauma in his life that caused him to be silent. The three temperaments I listed, timid, shy, and afraid, these all have the seed of shame. They are birthed from a place of shame. We learned from Genesis 3:10 that Adam hid because of shame.

And he said, I heard thy voice in the garden, and I was afraid, because I was naked; and I hid myself.

Where there is shame, silence is not far behind, and the person affected by this emotion will always live in secrecy.

I want to encourage all of you that are reading this book right now; it's your time to come out of hiding! What happened to you may not have been your fault, but when you start accepting it and hiding it because of shame, you made it your fault! I speak healing to your mind, your emotions and that every piece of your heart and identity that was broken because of the assault, the indictment, the abuse, I speak that you be mended 100% and made anew in your mind and in your heart. I declare that you will become the man God predestined you to be before the foundation of the world and you will no longer be plagued by guilt or shame. In Jesus' name!

DOMESTIC ABUSE TRAUMA

I recall the first trauma that taught me how to hide. As a little boy, I grew up in a very volatile home. As I referenced earlier, my father was a docile, non-talkative man until he had some libations. But he wasn't one of those individuals that just drank to have a social drink, to get a little feel good and be done. No, I don't ever recall a time ever that my father drank and did not get drunk. My father was the type of drinker that would fall out, urinate on himself, fight people (well his family) and become extremely belligerent.

My father's habit would start on Friday nights after work. He would not come directly home as he typically did Monday through Thursday. My family knew what that meant, that dad was out getting his drink on. He also wasn't necessarily the type of drinker who came home to drink. Although he did that on occasion, that wasn't his norm. Around 11pm, he walked through doors pissy drunk and coupled with the inebriation he would often be angry, the label given for this behavior was "angry drunk." Whatever did not go right for him that week at work or if something bothered him that my mother, me or one of my siblings did, he would not say anything while sober, but alcohol seem to be his power or courage drink, and he would let us have it with both barrels loaded as they say, was he got drunk.

It was during these times that my father would get into fist fights with my mother. I recall many times my mother and father starting off in a verbal argument, and because my mother was a talker, she had "a lot of mouth" as we used to say back in the day. My mother and father would be going at it, both cursing and raising their voices. My siblings and I would be somewhere in a corner hiding while trying to watch in fear, praying that what normally would happen would not happen this time. But as usual, my father would haul off and hit my mother somewhere on her body and the fight would ensue.

What I realized later as an adult man was my father would often hit my mother after the verbal arguing because my mother could outtalk him. But she couldn't out fight him. Once he hit my mother, my sister and brother would run into the room where the fight occurred and began to assist my mother as she would always reach for his private areas. Me, on the other hand, would stay back in the corner praying and wishing he would stop. This began the trauma as a little boy.

As I look back on the story and this history, the reason I never ran to assist my mother was because I had somehow internalized and begun to believe that it was my fault that my father was beating my mother. I grew up with this subliminal message that my father didn't like me, and because of his hatred for me, his anger was my fault. I carried these feelings for many years. The feelings came from messaging I heard from my mother, grandparents, family, friends, almost everyone. I was told I was my father's twin and that I looked exactly like him when he was my age. That would have been nice; however, I never believed my father liked himself. Because I believed he didn't like himself, in my little boy mind, I was convinced he didn't like me because I was his twin. I carried these feelings for as long as I could remember and every altercation, every time he got angry, I felt it had to do with him not liking himself and so I hid so he wouldn't have to see himself in me. The constant messaging that I heard and the heightened emotions were pervasive. It caused me to regularly hide or not be around him anytime he got inebriated.

What ingrained this notion in my head even greater was there was another incident where my father came home drunk after drinking at the bar or club, wherever he went. My father had a love for guns. He owned several rifles, and a 45 automatic. Well, this night, my father came home, and when he walked through the door after a period of being chilled in the kitchen, he said out of his mouth, "he was going to kill some niggas tonight." He goes to the closet that has his rifle and pulls it out. He makes us all go and sit in the dining room at the table. Fearful something bad is going to happen, we sat there trembling, and Dad takes his gun outside, but he begins walking around the house while we're in the dining room. He starts chanting, "he's going to kill some niggas tonight." Fear begins to paralyze all of us, and my mother tells us to start praying. But then suddenly, my father walks in the door, and when he reaches the threshold, he yells, "Peaches, where is Tony," without provocation! Everyone in my family knew I was afraid of my father and particularly when he got drunk, so my mother came out of the dining room so he wouldn't walk in there and tells my father that I'm upstairs, mind you, he's still chanting "I'm going to kill me some niggas tonight."

As my father goes upstairs looking for me, my mother grabbed all of us in our pj's, her car keys and we jetted out to her car. The family, as always, was protecting me from my father's drunken behavior. We got in my mom's car, and as usual, drove to the place we often went to when my father got into these drunken rages prior. We drove to the police station. Now in those days, if there were domestic violence in the home and they were called to the home, the police would come to the home and often make the aggressor leave the home until the aggressor sobered up. However, for fear of the unknown, we didn't stay that night waiting for the police. We drove to the station, but we didn't get out of the car and go into the station. We sat in the car and waited until my mom thought my father was asleep from his drunkenness. And as usual, when we got back home an hour or two later, dad was somewhere in the house sleeping the drunkenness off.

It was this constant drama that created trauma for me as a little lad. I would always internalize my father's behavior and resolve it to be I did something wrong that made him mad at my mother, or I did something wrong that made him drink, etc. These types of incidents went on for several years, and had it not been for Christ and his purpose stamped upon my life, I don't believe I would have made it out sane.

MOLESTATION TRAUMA

Because I began to allow trauma to defend me, I was cloaked in timidity. I seemed to be afraid of everything. The domestic trauma started causing me to have nightmares, and I was often afraid to be home alone because I would see images moving around in my brother and my bedroom. But I learned a valuable lesson that I understand now but didn't then. When trauma takes hold of you, it labels and imprisons you. Trauma will also make you prey to people who themselves are broken or have experienced trauma. I subscribe to the belief; broken people are drawn to broken people. As the saying goes, "birds of a feather flock together."

Broken people, it seems, will almost sniff out another broken or traumatized person. There were a few family members and friends that would frequent our home. Many of them were broken perpetrators of sexual abuse and molestations. It's amazing that my family never knew what skeletons hung in the closets of some of their family members and friends. But I was about to find out. Now I was a normal little boy who did things a little boy at my age did. At ten and eleven years old, my brother and I liked playing with fire engine trucks, our little green plastic Indian Chefs, dressing up like Cowboys and Indians, wrapping sheets around our necks and jumping off the top bunkbed pretending we could fly and watching cartoons on Saturday morning for several hours. I also liked girls and especially girls with long hair. If they allowed me to play in their hair, they became my girl. To this day, I'm still attracted to a woman with a beautiful head of hair; the longer, the better.

As a little boy, I was a skinny kid. If you coupled my skinniness with the domestic violence trauma and my timidity, I was prey for the child molesters. Understand child molesters don't always have a particular look. They don't wear a sign on their back exposing their heinous proclivity. They don't post ads on social media advertising they're looking for someone to abuse.

But what they do is come in familiar packaging. They develop friendships with you, attend the same church you do, preach from your pulpit, sing right next to you in the choir, and are family members. I stated all of this because many times when a person shares, they were molested, we start sizing them up and trying to identify who they were molested by. If a little boy or man says he was molested or raped, we automatically question, did a man molested him, and when a little girl or woman says she was molested or raped, we assume it was by a man.

Can anyone tell me why we assume or try to guess the gender of the perpetrator? What difference does it make? The reality is, it's all horrific and has the potential to scare the victim and cause them to become confused about their identity, their confidence and cloud their perspective on life. Can I suggest the next time someone confides in you and shares with you their story of rape, abuse, or molestation, don't inquire about who did it? Don't probe to get all the gory details about the incident, instead ask the victim if they're ok. If there is anything you can do, take the lead to listen with empathy and compassion. Pray with them, support them, and allow them to tell their story at their pace.

Now it's interesting because the molestation occurred when I was eleven, but the way the brain works, I suppressed it until I was thirty-one years of age. To the point I made at the beginning of this chapter, the brain is amazing, and it speaks to the awesome and magnificent God who created us. As the Psalms 139:14 says:

I will praise thee; for I am fearfully and wonderfully made: marvelous are thy works; and that my soul knoweth right well.

Because my little eleven-year-old mind could not handle the trauma of the abuse or process the threat made to my little mind by the perpetrator that if I told anyone my family would get hurt. No, this wasn't a movie of the week or something on Netflix. This was my experience at eleven years of age. But God covered me. I didn't have to deal with the fear that resulted from it, GOD hid it in the recesses of my mind... yea, I know I gave you some medical definitions at the beginning of this chapter how doctors postured how the brain deals with trauma, but I chose to look at it from another lens! It was God protecting my mind, putting a hedge around me, even when I didn't know that is what He was doing.

God knew I could not process it, so he let it come to the forefront of my brain when I could handle it. Hallelujah and my testimony today is that it did not cripple me, it did not define me, it did not confuse me about my identity. Why you may ask? Because of what Philippians 1:6 states:

Being confident of this very thing, that he which hath begun a good work in you will perform it until the day of Jesus Christ:"

When God created me, he made a promise that He would finish what He started in me. As I shared, it wasn't until I was thirty-one years old that the event came back to my mind, gushing out like a waterfall, detail after detail, moment by moment, into my conscious memory! As I sat on the couch at home with my wife watching an Oprah Winfrey episode about molestation, I began to cry like a baby and my wife asked what was wrong, and what happened to me at eleven years out began to spill out like a waterfall. It was amazing that I could share without shame, fear of rejection, or judgement. This trauma that was buried for twenty years as it spilled out, she offered safety and comfort in her arms.

I believe the beauty in sharing this story with you, however, is twofold. Some men are still silent about some horrific events that occurred in their formative years. It might not have been molestation. It could have been seeing one of their parents get murdered. It could have been experiencing a major accident that currently holds them hostage to traveling. It could have been seeing a sibling die and thinking it was their fault. It could have been feeling abandoned because their father or mother left the home after a divorce, and they never saw the parent again. Whatever caused the trauma, I've come to tell you that God has come to not arrest you but comfort you and provide you with a safe place to cry, to release the hurt, the disappointment, the fear, the regret.

But I also share my story to challenge women who may be reading this book. Are you a safe place for your husband, your fiancé, your boyfriend to cry, to mourn and release traumas and possible mistakes of his past? The place where he can reveal his heart and tell you the thing that may have broken him, that he has masked over and been silent about for years. Can you provide him comfort from the storm and allow him to expose the shame, and you cover him, not with judgement, but with your arms of love? The choice is your ladies.

CHURCH TRAUMA

I love church, and after I got filled with the Holy Spirit, I had such a hunger for God and for the things of God. I remember going to church and loving it. I loved the people, my pastor. I sang in the choir and ushered on the usher board. Church in my middle teen years became my life and a place of acceptance and joy. Again, I loved everything about church and God. One day a friend who sang next to me in the choir said during rehearsal that they wanted to tell me something about our pastor. Being naïve and excited about Jesus, I never thought in a million years that it would be something that would devastate and turn my world upside down.

Finally, I had found my identity and it was in Christ! I found a place I felt I belonged. I was coming out of my shyness, learning to dress. I loved wearing suits and even had a cute girlfriend at church my age. I was good! After rehearsal, I left church with my mom because she was waiting on me. I, therefore, had to tell my friend that I couldn't talk. They asked if they could call me later that evening once I got home, I said sure. Later that evening, they called the house, and I answered. The information they shared about my Pastor devastated me. It devastated me because my pastor was like the father I didn't have emotionally at home. He paid attention to me, taught me how to have swag in dressing, and most importantly, He provoked and cultivated my desire for God and His word. He was also a tremendously gifted orator, one who would mesmerize the congregation with his dynamic sermons and fiery style of preaching. He could hoop the saints out of their seats in ecstatic worship and dance. People would be speaking in tongues, dancing and running around the church! And this was every Sunday.

My pastor was my role model, who I desired to be just like. Well, what my friend told me not only devastated me, but it confused me. I didn't understand how a man so gifted and anointed could preach, lay hands on people, and they fall out, speak to demons in people and they'd come out. How could what my friend said be true? I didn't want to believe my friend, but I also didn't know what to do with the information. So, I shared it with my mother immediately. I thought to myself, she would know if this were true or false and know what to do about it. After telling my mother, I don't remember her having a negative response as I was telling her, nor do I remember her saying anything negative to me about our pastor. What she said was that she was going to pray about it and tell me later what we were going to do. The only direction she gave me was to not repeat to anyone what I was told by my friend.

Two days later, my mother informed me she had called to set up a meeting with our pastor to share with him what we were told. She told me that we both would be meeting with the pastor then said to me, we would be fine and not to worry because God would lead and guide us into all truth. When we met with our pastor, two weeks later, as my mother and I sat across from his big mahogany desk in his office at church, my mother began to share with him what I was told. I sat there about fifteen years old, watching my pastor's expression to see if he would get upset, angry or surprised. He showed no expression as my mother was talking. I began to think that what my friend told me about our pastor wasn't true.

After my mother finished sharing with our pastor what was said, my pastor never denied the information. He never got upset concerning the stories. What he did was present to us a question, more specifically, he presented the question to my mother. The question he asked my mother to my recollection was, "Sis Page, if your husband had a drinking problem, which he does, would you leave him or would you stay and love him through the process of deliverance and pray him through"? My mother said she would stay, love and pray him through it.

Well, the subliminal message was what we were told was true, but if we loved him, we would stay there to support him through the process of healing and deliverance. So, my mom and I left the church that day a little burdened (she was) but committed to staying at the church and praying our pastor through. We loved our pastor, and we felt he was genuinely sincere in what he told us. His final words to us as we walked out of his office was, he thanked us for sharing the information with him, and he encouraged us to stand with him in prayer for his deliverance and not share our conversation with anyone else.

We left the office resolved that we would support our pastor, pray him through and not leave the church. My mom shared with me the perspective that our pastor was just a man and that yes, he was gifted and anointed, but the anointing and gift, as the scripture said, is placed in an earthen vessel. Mom said that the pastor was human like us and that we should continue to pray and support him.

Later that evening after our meeting with our pastor I received a call from another friend who shared with me that our pastor had a meeting with all the leadership concerning my mother and I, and that we were being "silenced." He called to tell me that he couldn't talk to me anymore until the pastor publicly took us off silence. Now, if you don't know want silence is - in the Pentecostal church, it is when you are restricted by your pastor from talking to any of the members, and the members cannot talk to you for a period as determined by the pastor. During this silence period, you are still required to go to church, but you can't be involved in any activities in the church, and you have to sit in the back of the church when attending.

Here was another trauma I had to experience in a place that I thought was the best place in the world. As I stated earlier, I loved my church, my pastor and being involved. Now I couldn't sing in the choir, usher on the usher board and neither could my girlfriend talk to me.

Fifteen years of age, I was trying to process this event and the outcome. I felt like we were being punished for just telling the truth. We didn't do anything wrong. My mom nor I had planned to tell any other member about the incident. My mother told me explicitly not to tell anyone. So why did we have to be silenced?

What I learned later was that our pastor was trying to get ahead of the rumor we were told. By silencing us, it made us look like we had committed some type of public sin, which most people who were silenced had, i.e., girl getting pregnant out of wedlock or boys getting girls pregnant before marrying them or some other type of sexual sin that would be a public embarrassment. The rationale was these individuals were silenced because the sin they committed would eventually show publicly, and therefore they had to be punished publicly. Another terminology for being "silenced" was "to be sat down."

Of course, my mom and I did nothing of the sort. But the pastor cast a negative light on us by silencing us. If we told anyone what we heard about the pastor after the public announcement of us being silenced, it would appear as if we were lying on him in retaliation for silencing us.

We eventually left that church, and when we did start attending another church, my mindset on church had been so damaged that I resolved in myself that I wouldn't commit to another church again. I would go because I was still under my parent's roof and mom made me go, but I vowed not to get involve in church again. I would go just to check out the girls, sit and just profile! And for about three years, that is exactly what I did. But God has a way, when there is a mandate and call on your life… you can be like Jonah and run, but a whale is waiting.

I'm so glad God covered my mind, covered my destiny, and covered my identity.

The molestation was meant to silence me, and it did. My father's verbal abuse was to break me permanently, and it tried. The church hypocrisy was meant to make me cynical and condemnatory of church, and for a while, it did. But the muted little boy, afraid of his shadow, bruised spirit and confused mind, has stepped into his destiny with his mouth…using his words. This is my story, my testimony that I was muted, abused, confused and afraid, but God has redeemed the time and I am a living example of Joel 2:25.

And I will restore to you the years that the locust hath eaten, the cankerworm, and the caterpillar, and the palmerworm, my great army which I sent among you.

To the men holding this book in your hand now, don't allow the trauma of your past to stop you from triumphing today. God is not a respecter of persons, and just like he liberated me, he can and wants to do the same thing for you. If you don't have a safe place to release, ask God to send you someone you can trust with your brokenness and your trauma. Someone who will not trivialize your experiences but will walk with you and pray with you on your journey of recovery.

Yes, trauma is real, and it can have lasting effects, but I want you to remember, those of you that have a relationship with God the Father, he will keep you from falling and present you faultless in that day. Don't give up, my brother, on the journey. Push your way through. Allow the trauma and the memories of the trauma to come up and out. That is the only way you can be released from your past. Stop wrestling like Jacob and make your declaration today. You will be the man, the son, the husband, the businessman, the pastor or preacher God created you to be before the foundation of the world.

Brothers, I'm walking with you on this journey, and I believe in you. You will make it to your destiny I have no doubt. I'm assured because He made us a promise. Isaiah 43:2 hang your hope on this:

When thou passest through the waters, I will be with thee; and through the rivers, they shall not overflow thee: when thou walkest through the fire, thou shalt not be burned; neither shall the flame kindle upon thee.

~ **Questions For Reflection** ~

1. Take a moment and reflect on your trauma.
2. Are you ready to let the trauma go?
3. Is there someone you trust who you can tell your story?
4. Start seeing yourself free from the prison of trauma.

Chapter Five

ADAM, WHY ARE YOU SILENT?

Chapter Five

ADAM, WHY ARE YOU SILENT?

Specifically silent in times when our voice is needed the most. Why is this? Is it pervasive throughout the male population? Does it have to do with the cultures and environments in which we were reared? Does it have to do with our formative influences, or could it be a condition, a malady that predates our birth—a condition we were born with?

When we consider silence, the dictionary defines it as:

Noun: complete absence of sound.

Verb: prohibit or prevent from speaking.

What is preventing or prohibiting men from speaking? Does silence only deal with verbal communication? Could silence also be viewed as not being present in life? Not being present, participatory, or involved in the lives of the people who love us and perhaps even absent in our own lives.

Is silence a learned behavior, a type of male escapism, something that we as men have no control over? Is it a condition that can be understood, maybe even cured, is there a panacea? I suggest women would probably stand in line to purchase the medicine that would cure their husband, significant other, or male friend of their abject silence that has contributed to many arguments and frustrations in relationships, friendships, and life.

I advocate that male silence has a source and that there is a reason for the behavior. I profess the behavior can be understood and that there is hope for conversion. I am a living example and witness that silence does not have to be your permanent condition.

The issue of male silence predates us. We see in the Bible it originated with our first father, Adam. By all accounts, Adam was silent when he should have been a vociferous opponent tenacious to terminate the onslaught of their enemy! Adam should have been diligent to cover the precious gift given him by God. But instead, he was silent, mute, physically present, but perhaps emotionally and mentally absent. When backed up against a wall, called to step up to the plate and hit a homerun, secure victory and stability for our families, our societies, and ourselves, instead we run away in silence.

If you permit me, I invite you to go on this journey with me to not only investigate the rippling effects of Adam's silence and how it, even today, still affects men and women in relationships and our society. Open your hearts to learn and receive Adam's story, which affects our story.

ADAM WAS SILENT

The premise of this book is from Genesis 3:6, as I shared in the introduction. The Bible says that after Eve was deceived by Satan, she took some of the forbidden fruit … and ate it.

> *"She also gave some to her husband WHO WAS WITH HER, and he ate it."*

Adam, from all accounts, was standing right next to Eve when the serpent approached her, convinced her to disobey God? Wasn't Adam listening to every word, but he chose not to speak a word? He was silent. Adam was not only silent with the serpent, but he was also silent with Eve. He never reminded her of God's word. He never called her to a larger vision. He did not join his wife in the battle with the serpent. He passively listened to her speak rather than speaking with her in mutual respect and partnership.

I'm not suggesting that Adam should have spoken for Eve, but why didn't he speak to Eve? She was bone of his bone and flesh of his flesh. Many men make this same mistake in relationships. Instead of speaking to our wives, our girlfriends, we talk at them or stop talking all together. Both men and women were created in God's image to speak. This example of Adam being quiet was his first sin.

Adam disobeyed by failing to speak with the serpent and with his wife. He was absent and passive. His silence was symbolic of his refusal to be involved with Eve. And God punished Adam for his silence. Genesis 3:17

And unto Adam he said, Because thou hast hearkened unto the voice of thy wife, and hast eaten of the tree, of which I commanded thee, saying, Thou shalt not eat of it: cursed is the ground for thy sake; in sorrow shalt thou eat of it all the days of thy life;

God punished Adam for eating the forbidden fruit. But he also punished him for listening to his wife. Adam's disobedience was a process. Adam was silent and then ate from the tree. His disobedience did not begin with his eating but with his silence. Disobeying God was a result of retreating from his wife. It was a silent man who eventually broke God's command.

SILENCE IS DEADLY

Like every man, we are silent, just like Adam was silent. Sometimes we are silent in confusion when our wives ask us to share the smallest part of ourselves. How do you respond? When she cries, do you get angry with her? Do her tears frighten you because you don't know what to do with them? When she tells you something is wrong, that you've done something wrong, do you try to defend yourself to the bitter end. If she finds fault with you, do you, in exchange, try to find ten things wrong with her because you refuse to be wrong. You use words, you speak, but is it for the purpose of destroying the relationship as the serpent did in the garden.

But if your wife was able to scratch beneath the surface of your anger, she would find that you are ashamed of what is inside of you. What if you shared your most intimate thoughts, dreams, and doubts and she rejects you? Would that make you go back into silence?

Silence is not golden. It is deadly. Adam's silence was lethal. It brought death. When you are silent, what does it do to your wife? It points the finger at her and blames her for wanting too much. Like Adam, I wanted to blame my ex-wife for all the chaos of our marriage and the reason it failed. Remember, didn't Adam say in Genesis 3:12:

And the man said, The woman whom thou gavest to be with me, she gave me of the tree, and I did eat said "the woman you

Blaming her, Adam thought he could take the responsibility off of himself and put it on Eve. The principle we must be aware of, however, is <u>when we are silent, it brings the one connected to us into our confusion and ultimate sin of disobedience.</u>

We learn a valuable lesson from Adam's silence. Because he was silent, it changed the original order of headship and the dynamic of male/female relationships. Eve was never created to provide for Adam but to be a helpmeet. God created Adam to provide for Eve. When Adam went silent, it killed the original order of male/female relationships. And now man's silence becomes his defense against making another mistake again.

The author of Genesis is a storyteller. He has revealed the plot and the problem in the first three chapters. The next forty-seven chapters play out the same theme in countless fascinating stores. As with any good story, Genesis repeats the same themes and events. And the theme of masculine silence appears again and again.

As I have mentioned in earlier chapters Abraham, Isaac and Jacob all choose to be silent and oblivious, absent, and forgetful. And they consistently get into trouble whenever they choose silence over involvement or forgetting over remembering.

What is the lesson for us men as we see Adam go silent? That silence never solves the problem. Men were made in the image and likeness of God; he was created to be an image-bearer and to project God's image on the earth. The moment Adam stops talking, he stops imaging God... he stops representing God.

THE CALL TO REMEMBER

When men chose silence, we chose to stop remembering what God said. It is ironic that most men are known for their silence. Their children rarely learn about their past – experiences, failures, and struggles. Instead of passing something on to the children positively, the man remains silent. He acts as if he has no memory. Why?

It is easy for a man not to remember because he uses the lack of his memory as his excuse to not be accountable. Therefore, silence is often easier for men.

Think about it, for us to sin conveniently, we must purposefully forget God's word. Sinful choices require that we forget what God said in His word. Forgetting is more than forgetting where you placed your car keys. It is an active and willful choice – a refusal to remember. This is what Paul is referencing in Romans 1:23 when Paul paints a vivid picture of what happened when men exchanged the glory of the immortal God for images made to look like mortal man.

The Bible says, "God gave them over in the sinful desire of their hearts to sexual impurity." Why? As verse 28 advises, because they did not think it worthy to retain the knowledge of God, he gave them over to a depraved mind to do what ought not be done. The people described in the text chose intentionally to forget God.

This is what it means when we go silent men, to make a conscious decision to forget God and not remember what He said. I can't be silent any longer because I have decided to remember God's word, and in remembering His word, I am remembering who He called me to be.

Who are you? You don't know, or you've forgotten? Yes, you may have experienced trauma, and yes, you may have been mislabeled, misunderstood, and misidentified, but today, I want to encourage you! REMEMBER!

The silence of Adam is a wake-up call for us men. Adam had everything he could ever want, property, a fine wife, the best food, and a job where all his employees obeyed him. But how did he lose it all. He chose not to remember. His silence was a sign of forgetting what God told him to do. In Genesis 1:28, God said to Adam and Eve:

Be fruitful, and multiply, and replenish the earth, and subdue it: and have dominion over the fish of the sea, and over the fowl of the air, and over every living thing that moveth upon the earth.

Five things Adam was called to remember:

- **Be fruitful** – plant.
- **Multiply** – bring increase to what you've planted.
- **Replenish** – restore, restock, pour back into what you plant.
- **Subdue** – keep what has been given under control.

All Adam had to do was remember what he was told. If he would have spoken to Eve, interrupted her conversation with the serpent and reminded her that the serpent had to come under her control and not she come under his. If only he had told her this one thing, He would have displayed for Eve the importance of remembering.

REMEMBER WHAT GOD SAID

To the men who will be healed by this book and the women who will be enlightened to this liberating truth. Living life in silence is not your destiny man, as the old mothers of the church would say, "this is not your portion."

John 8:36 declares:

> *"If the Son therefore shall make you free, ye shall be free indeed."*

~ Questions For Reflection ~

1. Take a moment and reflect on what you forgot that God said about you.
2. Take a moment to write down what God said.
3. Tell somebody else what you remember God saying?
4. Meditate on what God said.

Chapter Six

FATHERS & MENTORS

Chapter Six

FATHERS & MENTORS

W*e continue to walk the path to maturity when we admit how deeply we long for a father, a man who walks ahead of us, letting us know what is possible and calling us to follow, and a brother, a peer whose struggles, and compassion encourages us to make ourselves known to him as we walk together. When the reality hits you, as it will for most men, that we have neither father nor brother, the overwhelming disappointment can either turn into bitterness or it can drive us to seek God with all our hearts and to become fathers and brothers for other men. For those few who know the joy of being well fathered and richly brothered, the calling is not merely to enjoy these blessings but to provide the same one for others.*

If men today are willing to look into darkness, to remember God and then to speak words that bring life to others, if they are willing to walk the steep, narrow, long path toward true masculinity, then perhaps our children will enter their adult years blessed with an older generation of mentors, men who father well as they walk with their brothers toward home.

"Fathers Shape Us"

The word father describes one who gives life or who creates, originates, exemplifies, or finds something. The power of a father can shape and mold the identity of the child. I believe that a father has the power to give his children something that no one else can. My belief comes from the pattern that was established since the beginning of time. When examined in scripture the father has both physical and spiritual authority over his children and charged to speak into their lives. We see this in Genesis 49:1-27.

Jacob commands the blessing over his 12 sons.

"And Jacob called unto his sons, and said, gather yourselves together, that I may tell you that which shall befall you in the last days. Gather yourselves together, and hear, ye sons of Jacob; and hearken unto Israel your father. "Genesis 49:1-2

The current world we live in, unfortunately, fathers don't seem to be that important anymore. Fathers are marginalized, minimized, and often misunderstood. Why is this? What has happened with the role of the father and its importance in society?

I present this for your consideration because I believe one of the reasons why men go silent is because we don't see fathers present in homes nor hear their voices speaking over us. Could it be that fathers are no longer a necessity but an anomaly? It has been said that America is rapidly becoming a fatherless society, or perhaps more accurately, an absentee father society. The importance and influence of fathers in families have significantly declined since the Industrial Revolution.

David Popenoe, a professor of sociology at Rutgers University, recorded "the percentage of American children living apart from their biological fathers will reach 50% by the next century." He argued that it is "this massive erosion of fatherhood" that contributes mightily to many of the major social problems of our time.

Data has shown that a fatherless child has a risk factor of two to three times that of fathered children for a wide range of negative outcomes, including dropping out of high school, giving birth as a teenager, and becoming a juvenile delinquent, to name a few.

We are not just experiencing the loss of fathers, but the idea of fatherhood is eroding. It is interesting that society as a whole does not doubt the fundamental importance of mothers but increasingly question, are fathers really necessary. One article I read said that the father role is now being viewed as merely a social role that other people can substitute in, i.e., partners, stepfathers, uncles, aunts, and grandparents can play.

I submit, being a good father isn't about what kind of parent you are as much as it is about what kind of person you are. What kind of character do you have? How do you approach life and your responsibilities as a father?

Fathers have an innate ability to influence their children and the community around them. I subscribe to the premise that fathers have power. Even though my father wasn't necessarily a positive role model, he did teach me what not to be. Being a father is not about physical power or being bigger and stronger than the wives and kids, but the power of fathers is a generational power that God has endowed us with! It is power that allows us to affect people's lives positively or negatively, for good or evil, for hundreds of years. A father will impact people he doesn't even know and will never meet.

A Father's Voice

Something deeply important is that fathers understand the power of their voice is a shadow or an image of God, the Father's voice himself! Ask yourself a few questions; do you know the power of your voice? Is your voice doing what it needs to do in your children's lives? Is your voice one of love, truth, and grace, yet authoritative, conferring blessings upon them? Or is your voice harsh, critical, condemning and potentially lethal?

Your voice has a certain kind of weight in the ears of your children. This is something that needs to be cultivated. A quote I read said, "Words have an awesome impact. The impression made by a father's voice can set in motion an entire trend of life." Have you ever asked yourself how much weight your voice carries in your home? Do you think your voice matters?

When you say something, how are you stewarding the power and the gravity of your voice? Maybe this was God's design, that fathers carry the family not only by providing, protecting, and professing but also by prophesying... speaking into them their purpose and destiny. I'm grateful as a father that I was mindful and intentional about the words I spoke into my daughters. I failed as a husband, but I purposed not to fail as a father. As they were growing up and because I wasn't physically in the home, I needed to be overly communicative. My words, tone, and frequency were key. Did I get it right all the time? No, I didn't, but I was always mindful to keep working at it.

Because I was silent with my ex-wife for many years, and ultimately was one of the reasons for the demise of our marriage. I knew, however, I couldn't be silent with my girls. I accepted the fact that part of their validation came from my words and consistency in their lives. My goal was to give them what I didn't get. When speaking with them whether over the phone, in person and now with modern technology, via facetime, and texting, my words are deliberate and intentional - they are aimed at building them and not demolishing them.

I wrote this chapter because I want men to understand how important having a father present and being a father is. If your story is similar to mine and you didn't have an affirming father or one that was engaged in your life, accept that as your truth, process it but then move on to determine how you can be a better father to your children despite what you didn't get. Don't allow what you were deprived of to handicap you and become your excuse for poor fathering. It is within your power to be a great dad. No, it may not have been modeled in front of you, but it's in you! Ask God to connect you with other fathers who can assist in the process. But be willing to receive and grow from what you don't know. As men, if we aren't careful, we will dress up shame to appear as we don't need anything or anyone's help.

But let me share a little secret, shame as I shared earlier is from the seed of fear but it is also one of the faces of pride. Don't be a victim of pride and end up as Proverbs 16:18 declares:

> **Pride goeth before destruction, and an haughty spirit before a fall.**

One of the definitions for haughty is arrogance, and men, we are good at being arrogant in our ignorance.

MENTORS

This is where mentors come in. Men, when we don't know something, reach out for help and support. Become a part of a men's group at church, a father's support group, a men's accountability group. Believe it or not, there are many available groups that we can be a part of and grow. You may not be aware of them for lack of research. Let me help you out! Check them out:

https://fathers4kids.com/

https://www.fatherhood.org/

https://fathersrightsmovement.us/

http://blackfathersfoundation.org

Doing this requires some vulnerability on your part, but the vulnerability will be worth it! In connecting with some of these opportunities, you will not only gain tools that can assist you in being a better father, but you will also develop new relationships, as the bible describes, "iron sharpening iron." I find it interesting that men have difficulty forming healthy relationships with other men.

Now, I don't say this from a place of arrogance or that it has been easy for me, but what I've learned in my life is that it was necessary for me to develop healthy relationships with other men for my betterment. I recall a time about thirty-five years ago when Bishop Jakes had his Manpower Conferences. One year, three friends and I, attended the conference together. Two of the friends I knew from Bible College and the third friend I met for the first time at the conference. We all stayed together in a suite at the Embassy Suites. During the conference, Bishop Jakes said something that was not only eye-opening but resonated with truth. He made this comment – *"men don't have an issue with other men seeing them naked, the issue comes in not knowing what the man thinks about your nakedness when he walks away."*

I will never forget that statement because it spoke the truth of my experiences with other men in the past. I always tried to prove I was as strong, athletic, or masculine as the next man.

Constantly caught up in this merry-go-round of jockey for position and pontificating, when what I actually needed was a brother or two that I could have covenant with. A company of brothers with whom I could feel safe, vulnerable, yet my masculinity not be labeled as weak.

Do you remember the group of men I mentioned I attended the Manpower Conference with? Well, after one of the sessions at the conference, we went back to the room and did an exercise that I will never forget. It was this exercise that set my expectation for what to look for in real male friendships.

I don't remember who initiated this exercise but one of the brothers said let's tell each other all our dark secrets, weaknesses, frailties, mistakes, etc., and after we hear the negative things about one another, each brother will take a moment to speak into each other potential and destiny. To speak words of affirmation, possibilities, strengths, and opportunities. To speak into who we could and would become. I still get emotional thinking about the brotherhood that developed from that. For me, it was transformative. It was the first time I trusted my secrets, failures, weakness with another brother and did not feel judged! After hearing my darkness, the brothers didn't focus on the dark stuff but began to speak into my brilliance, and light!

Believe it or not, we brothers, although we don't talk often, when we connect, the bond is still there, thirty five years later because real intimacy was shared amongst us. We allowed each other to look in and see, not our representative, but see the broken, scared little boy and speak life. For us, it was truly a David & Jonathan experience.

This is what I wish for my brothers reading this book, that you will find a Jonathan to your David who will cover your nakedness and not expose you but allow you to heal in safety and honor! A mentor who will take time to hear you, understand you, strengthen you, and speak into you.

Mentors can provide you an opportunity to grow. Grow by being challenged and supported, where you can gather wisdom from other men and move forward powerfully through the transitions and passages of your life. Men, we don't have to suffer in isolation, it isn't healthy, and happiness cannot be acquired alone. God created us for relationship. When we try to do life on our own, statistics show, we end up medicating the pain and filling the void with vices that turn into addictions, and we are left with unfulfilled lives.

I believe the men reading this book desire to live full, productive, and satisfying lives. I believe you want to positively impact your families, your churches, and the world. I believe if you decide on finding a mentor, open yourself to the possibility - your family will benefit, your work will benefit, your world will benefit, you will benefit. Another resource to consider is:

https://mankindproject.org/men-helping-men/

If we don't seek to transform our pain, we'll just transfer it to others.

~ Questions For Reflection ~

1. Take a moment and reflect on your relationship or lack thereof with your father.
2. What will you do about the relationship with your father to make it better, if possible?
3. Have you ever thought about mentorship?
4. What are your fears about finding a mentor?

Chapter Seven

SPEAK TO THE ROCK

Chapter Seven

SPEAK TO THE ROCK

"Our words have creative power. With words, we can speak blessings over our future." Joyce Meyer

I have a strong attraction to words. I think it is because, for so many years, I was silent. So now, when words are spoken, I pay attention closely to what is being said, specifically the words. Not only do I focus on words, but I also focus on tone and inflection. And when possible and talking with someone in person, I focus on expression.

I think that's because for so long, I didn't share or speak my feelings. I did not express what I thought through my words. It is interesting because the scripture says in Proverbs 18:21

Death and life are in the power of the tongue: and they that love it shall eat the fruit thereof.

This scripture gives the implication that words spoken from our mouths can produce life or death. I believe this to be true.

As a young boy growing up into an adolescent, teenager, young man, and adult man who eventually became a husband and father, words became very significant for me. Words of affirmation, impartation, guidance, and even correction. They became important because as shared, there was a deficient of these things when I was growing up.

Later on, I got the revelation that not only my voice is important, but the words I speak are important. In this chapter, I want to talk to men about the importance of your words because your words shape your world. We become the words we read when we speak them. They shape the pattern of our thoughts, affect our moods, and influence our world. We BECOME the words with which we surround ourselves. Let's look at this principle from a biblical perspective. John 1:1

In the beginning was the Word, and the Word was with God, and the Word was God

What John is revealing to us is that when God wanted to reveal himself to mankind, He wrapped himself up in flesh, came into the earth in the form of Jesus the Christ, and called him, "the Word." The term "the word" is insightful because in studying the text, you understand that the translation of "word" in Greek is "*logos,*" which in the simplest definition means "*spoken expression or statement.*"

We see this principle starting in Genesis 1 when God created, He spoke "words" … for the Bible says and "God said." Eight times from Genesis 1:1 to 1:26. God created simply by the power of His Word.

When God desired to express Himself, He spoke words, and those words created, made something happen. We begin to understand this partnership by drawing an analogy to how our own thoughts and words reach into the physical world. When we desire to command something to happen in the world around us, we must first conceive the idea in our minds. No one can see our thoughts. They are invisible, yet they certainly exist. Without our thoughts, we could purpose to do nothing at all.

If our thoughts are to become visible in some way, they must move from the invisible realm of our mind and into the physical world. The progression from invisible to visible requires we transfer our invisible thoughts into a spoken command. The brain communicates our thoughts to our mouth, where it becomes *logos*: spoken words. Once the spoken word leaves our mouth, it enters the physical world and yields its intended effect. This simple analogy helps explain how God the Father worked with God the Son (*i.e.*, the Word) to establish Creation.

The importance of understanding, like God, our words create. As men, when we determine that we will no longer be silent but speak. What will we speak and how will we speak it? It is important that we are mindful of this. Often when you are in a situation where you've been silent for so long and you have permission and a freedom to start doing what you hadn't done in a long time, you overindulge. Open the flood gates and go wild.

The first thing that is important to understand is speaking is the gateway to relationship. Your silence for a long time was the gatekeeper. The Hebrew Bible teaches us that our words usher us out of silence and connects us with God and one another. Being present in your words is a potent opportunity to bring life into areas where death reigns. But with this new opportunity, there will be levels of trepidation and uncertainty because you are using a tool you had stopped using or never used.

As you begin to express yourself through words, be mindful that people may also be a little apprehensive of receiving you. They may not readily receive your words because it will sound foreign to them. Stay the course. This is your opportunity to introduce them to the new you, the expressive, present you! You are on the right track going in the right direction. It may just take some people a moment to get on the track with you.

I write this chapter to prepare you. As excited as I am about your conversion from being mute to being vocal and present, I must be honest and make you aware of potential negative responses. In the beginning, when I found my voice and started talking. I said everything I thought and felt … I expressed myself in words. If I thought someone was unattractive, I would say it. If I thought someone wasn't so smart, I would say it. But what I began to see was my words were starting to push people away and silence them, that I wasn't speaking life but death.

I'm reminded of the story in Numbers 20:8-11 where God gave Moses' instructions to speak to the rock, and instead of speaking, he struck the rock.

"Take the staff, and assemble the congregation, you and Aaron your brother, and tell the rock before their eyes to yield its water. So you shall bring water out of the rock for them and give drink to the congregation and their cattle." And Moses took the staff from before the Lord, as he commanded him. Then Moses and Aaron gathered the assembly together before the rock, and he said to them, "Hear now, you rebels: shall we bring water for you out of this rock?" And Moses lifted up his hand and struck the rock with his staff twice, and water came out abundantly, and the congregation drank, and their livestock. (ESV)

God instructed Moses to speak to the rock and out of it would flow water. But instead, he struck the rock multiple times. Did water flow from the rock as God said it would? It did, because God's word will always be fulfilled. However, the result of Moses disobeying God and hitting the rock was he would not see what God promised, the Promise Land. Now the obvious lesson is that all disobedience is sin and that God had given Moses clear instructions to follow.

There is a theological interpretation of this story that Moses' problem wasn't that he misinterpreted God or thought that since he'd hit the rock before as instructed in Exodus 17 that it was okay to do it again. Rather, Moses was utterly rejecting God and trying to take control.

- Moses was violent. He struck the rock *twice* when God just said to speak to it.

- Moses was usurping God's place. He said to the people, "hear now, you rebels shall we bring water for you out of this rock?" Moses didn't say "God will bring water out of this rock for you." He took God's place and assured them that he would do it for them.

In addition, the thought is when the Lord instructed Moses to strike the rock in Exodus 17, He intended to establish a picture of Christ as our Redeemer. The Bible repeatedly says in Psalms and Isaiah that Christ is our Rock and Cornerstone struck for our sake, and He will bring forth streams of living water (i.e., salvation). Moreover, Hebrews says Christ died once for all and no further sacrifice for sins is required.

Moses was instructed to strike the rock in the desert <u>only once</u> as it was a picture of Jesus being sacrificed once to bring us salvation. When we get to Numbers 20, the Lord instructed Moses to only speak to the rock to preserve the picture created in Exodus 17. When Moses chose to strike the rock a second time instead, he disrupted the picture created in Exodus 17. It is said that Moses, from a theological lens, confused and distorted the picture of the sacrifice of Jesus Christ, our rock.

But if you will allow me, I saw this text from another lens that specifically applies to us men speaking and the importance of the way we speak. Now I will go on record and admit to all my Bible scholars I am taking some liberties and taking the text out of context. My goal, however, is not to impose another interpretation on the text but to extrapolate a principle from the story.

God told Moses to speak to the rock and water would flow from it, instead, Moses struck the rock twice. Men, your words are important, absolutely, but so is your tone. I'm sure you've heard, "it's not what you say but how you say it." I challenge you, men, become stewards of your words and masters of your tone. Sometimes our message is not received because of how we say it.

Having worked in Human Resources for over eighteen years, I facilitated many leadership trainings. One of the trainings I did focused on communication. Psychology Prof. Albert Mehrabian of the University of California in Los Angeles suggests in one of his studies that in communication, a speaker's words are only a fraction of his efforts. The pitch and tone of his voice, the speed and rhythm of the spoken word, and the pauses between those words may express more than what is being communicated by words alone. Further, his gestures, posture, pose and expressions usually convey a variety of subtle signals. These non-verbal elements can present a listener with important clues to the speaker's thoughts and feelings and thus substantiate or contradict the speaker's words. The rule is called:

7-38-55 Rule of Personal Communication

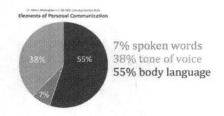

The rule states 7 percent of meaning is communicated through spoken word, 38 percent through tone of voice, and 55 percent through body language. In the world of effective communication, 93 percent of meaning is communicated non-verbally. Your tone of voice and body language are much more important than what you say with just your words.

Men, now that you're regaining your voice and/or on the road to recovering your voice, body language and tone is extremely important as you seek to reach and engage your audiences. Your audiences may consist of your wives, girlfriend, children, employer, colleagues, parishioners, and pastors, to name a few. The key to reaching them will encompass your words matching your body language and tone.

How many of you talk or respond with a grunt, a nod, a frown, or raised eyebrow or body language that communicates you're closed off or not receiving the sender's message. Body language like folded arms, crossed legs, etc.? Men don't only focus on your words but pay attention to your body language. We communicate for the purpose of exchange. Studies have shown that men and women communicate for different reasons. Women communicate to express their feelings, but men communicate to seek understanding.

I remember when I was married, and even today, anytime a woman said to me, "I want to talk" or "we need to talk," I immediately thought there was something wrong that either I did or needed to fix. That is the wiring of our brain, men!

Men and women also have different conversational styles. Women tend to talk faster when they get excited, and we men sometimes struggle with finding the right words and our responses may be delayed. Women attach feeling to words. Men, we typically don't attach emotions to words.

Whatever the case, men and women, when you speak, it does matter and it's important! Communication involves a sender, a recipient and it's about information being exchanged. When communicating, seek to:

1. Understand (empathy)
2. Not Judge
3. Be aware of body language
4. Listen and Engage

And remember:

The biggest communication problem is we do not listen to understand. We listen to reply.

~ Questions For Reflection ~

1. Take a moment and reflect on how you communicate.
2. What areas do you need to work on in your communication?
3. Are you aware of your non-verbal communication?
4. How well do you listen?

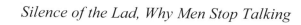

Chapter Eight

RELATIONSHIPS

Chapter Eight

RELATIONSHIPS

What would life be without relationships?

Healthy relationships--those that are mutually caring and giving--are necessary for personal success. Everyone needs someone to learn from and share ideas with. Good relationships offer understanding when you fail, confidence when you're in doubt, and celebration as you go through life. They also allow you opportunities to grow, give, to mentor, and to share.*

I wholeheartedly believe that healthy relationships are the nectar of human existence. In the amazing mind of God, he did not create Adam to be alone. In fact, Moses eavesdrops on God's conversation with himself and writes in Genesis 2:18:

> *"And the LORD God said, It is not good that the man should be alone; I will make him an help meet for him."*

Interesting because this text is the first bit of tension in the Genesis narrative. Something is **not good**. Let me reiterate that the determiner of what is "good" and "not good" is not the collective agreement of a society but God Himself. What God declares good is indeed good and what He declares not good is indeed not good.

For consideration let me give you four reasons why this was not good.

The Imago Dei

First, Adam alone doesn't fully reflect the image of God.

One Theologian stated that man alone, nor the man and woman together represented the image of God, but it was the whole of humanity, his children, his offspring that fully revealed God's image.

God's image is much too rich for it to be fully realized in a single human being, however richly gifted that human being might be.

God's image is unfolded in its depth and riches in all of humanity.

God shows Adam that he has a need: it is not good for him to be alone. And one of the reasons it's not good for Adam to be alone is because one single man on the whole planet doesn't accurately reflect who God is!

Procreation

Secondly, Adam cannot be fruitful and multiply alone. It is not good for him to be alone because the human race does not come into existence with only Adam. Look at the amazing God; inside of Adam from the beginning was the DNA for female. God didn't just merely use his rib, but God designed men to provide an X (female) or a Y (male) chromosome to the woman's X chromosome to come up with either (XY) male or (XX) female. For God's glory and our good, two genders are required for the human race to exist and procreate future generations.

Unity

Thirdly, God made a woman to complement Adam. That's not compliment like, "WOW Adam, aren't you so strong!" It's **complement** with an 'e,' which has the idea of completing. The phrase "*fit for him*" literally means something like "*one opposite him.*" God was going to make one like Adam but yet opposite of Adam.

I submit to you here is one reason why love is beautifully expressed when we love those "not like us."

Marriage between a man and a woman is really about God allowing two opposite people of His design, coming together with differences of opinion, different thoughts, different habits, different histories, coming together and becoming one! God didn't create clones - but someone who is different and has a different role – someone who **complements** you. Eve was to be a **helper** to Adam, which doesn't imply <u>her inferiority</u> or <u>Adam's superiority</u> but highlights the need for both male and female to complement one another in order to fulfill God's good design for humanity.

So, I think it's important to highlight that God did not only give Adam a wife so that they could populate the earth, although important, but so that Adam could understand the God-kind-of love. God gave him somebody to love. When we look at love in the way God designed it, love is the opposite of selfishness. Many people try to have relationships, but they remain selfish and self-centered. I'm here to tell you, that relationship will be short-lived. The foundation of a God-ordained relationship is that it exhibits the God-kind-of-love. May I suggest to you, the primary thing that will keep a marriage together is not good sex, it is not liking the same things, it is not having a lot in common or never having a disagreement but having the God-kind-of-love. It is the love that seeks not its own! 1 Corinthians 13:5 says it like this:

...or rude. It does not insist on its own way; it is not irritable or resentful;

It is the kind of love that will make sacrifices for the sake of the relationship. The sacrifice isn't made because you don't want your spouse to be mad at you or you're tired of fussing. No, it is the love that says, I want my marriage to work and because I want my marriage to work, I will sacrifice my opinion and the privilege of being right to be in harmony. We have often thought that harmony is everyone thinking the same way and doing the same thing exactly the same. But I think we can learn a thing or two from music theory.

In music theory, harmony is **when two sounds are played in unison**. If you play the notes C – E – G melodically, you get individual notes from the C major scale. If you play C – E – G harmonically, at the same time, you get a C major chord....

This understanding from music theory helps us to see clearly what complement really means in a relationship. It's when he brings all his experiences, personality, gifts, talents, material gain, he brings it all to the table and submits it. While she does the same, bringing all her experiences, personality, gifts, talents, and material gain to the table and submits them. In submitting what they bring to the table (*the table represents the relationship*) produces harmony/unison. If you've ever heard an orchestra play it's amazing because you may hear the distinctions of the various instruments, i.e., the flute, horn, bass, piano, etc., but when they all play from the same sheet of music, it is harmonious! That is the beauty of relationships!

But also understand mankind was created to be a social being. This should not surprise us when we understand the triune nature of God. Our triune God has never been alone! God is eternally relational. He is not in need of humanity to express His relationality as some have proposed. And so, it's no surprise that God would not just make one person but people.

And this idea leads me to my last point on why it's not good for man to be alone:

Worship

Fourthly, from the very beginning, God has been about <u>a people</u>. Individuals can worship God, but the beauty of God's design is that He is after <u>a people</u> for Himself.

The gospel message at the core is not merely about "me" but "us." Christ came to redeem <u>a people</u>. Titus 2:14:

> ***Who gave himself for us, that he might redeem us from all iniquity, and purify unto himself a peculiar people, zealous of good works.***

To love God involves loving others, specifically loving others, not like yourself. I've often questioned could one of the reasons why our churches are so empty is because we are so narcissistic in our approach to sharing the gospel of Jesus Christ. We only look for and approach people who look like us, dress like us, think like us or have the same socioeconomic status as us to share Jesus with.

Because of our selfishness, it's easy to love people just like us. It's harder to love those who think and act differently than we do. What I'm getting at here is that God is glorified in a diverse people surrendered to Him in worshipful obedience. God didn't clone Adam. He made a woman who was both like Adam and not like Adam so that He could have a diverse people to worship Him. From the beginning of creation, we were never meant to worship alone.

Let us praise God, who is the great designer. How wonderful are the two genders of humanity! How wonderful it is that we were not made to be alone. How good God is to His creation. How good God is in calling a people to himself.

I wrote this chapter to express the importance of all types of relationships. Those of you that are single and desiring to be married, first be honest with yourself and answer this simple question - are you ready for marriage, or are you still selfish? I've had to ask myself those questions. Truth be told, after being divorced for over fifteen years, I'm still single because I have some selfishness issues. I remember while being married that I was selfish. I was more focused on having my way than having the marriage. And just being transparent, since I've told you so much already, another reason my marriage failed was because of selfishness. I think my ex-wife struggled with some selfishness being the youngest child and I definitely had some selfish ways. So much so that at the end of the day, the focus wasn't the marriage but having our own way. We read in Matthew 12 about a house divided against itself cannot stand, but do we really believe it?

I will say as a divorced man, don't go into a relationship if you aren't ready to make the relationship a priority. Marriages survive, I believe, because you go into them understanding you both are to **complement** each other, not **compliment** each other! The job description is to create harmony. My ex-wife and I complimented each other aesthetically. I used to say all the time our family looked like we could have posed for the church fan. But appearance doesn't make a marriage last.

Secondly, I wrote this chapter because it is important to understand that God created us because He desired a people through which He could show Himself strong in. 2 Chronicles 16:9

For the eyes of the LORD run to and fro throughout the whole earth, to shew himself strong in the behalf of them whose heart is perfect toward him.

We weren't created to live on an island and to do life alone. Our God is relational, and therefore, He created others for us to have relationships with. Let me explain what I mean when I say God is a relational God. It simply means God feels and is moved to action by what He feels. John 3:16 screams this truth:

For God so loved the world that he gave his one and only Son, that whoever believes in him shall not perish but have eternal life.

What God felt was the "so loved," and this feeling moved Him to act "He gave." The Bible is replete with describing God as feeling - compassion, having great delight, showing lovingkindness, tender mercy, regretting, being longsuffering, and the list goes on.

My point, He is a relational God, and He made us in His image and after His likeness. Stop allowing yourself to not feel or pretend you don't care about others. We were placed on this earth to bear one another up, strengthen one another, and care for one another.

If you have been hurt and it has caused you to close-up the bowels of your compassion, ask God to heal your emotions and heal your memory so the hurt that someone else inflicted upon you twelve or twenty-five years ago, will no longer poison your spirit and infect your heart. The same God that took the poison out of the snake that bite Paul in Acts 28:5 will do the same for you.

We were created to worship God together in the beauty of holiness. It's time to show the world what the Ekklēsia really looks like. Until we come into the unity of the faith with one another, we will not be able to mandate the legislation of heaven into the earth's realm! Isaiah 1:18:

Come now, and let us reason together, saith the Lord: though your sins be as scarlet, they shall be as white as snow; though they be red like crimson, they shall be as wool.

~ Questions For Reflection ~

1. Take a moment and check your relationships.
2. Whomever you have an issue with, contact them to heal.
3. Are you selfish? Correct it.
4. Have you prayed and asked God to heal your heart and the memories of past hurts?

Chapter Nine

YOU ARE A SPEAKING SPIRIT

$$\mathcal{C}hapter\ \mathcal{N}ine$$

YOU ARE A SPEAKING SPIRIT

Genesis 2:7,

"and man became a living soul, "*a speaking spirit***." God created man in His own image with the capacity to speak and communicate.**

A leading neurosurgeon has said that the speech center in the brain exercises dominion over the whole central nervous system. He also stated that this is a recent discovery. He said that you could cause different parts of the body to respond with stimuli to corresponding parts of the human brain. However, when the speech center is stimulated, the entire central nervous system responds. This means that when anyone says, "I am weak," the speech center sends out the message to the whole body to prepare to be weak.

This must be the reason God said,

"Let the weak say, I am strong," Joel 3:10.

By Your Words

For in many things we offend all. If any man offend not in word, the same is a perfect man, and able also to bridle the whole body.

(James 3:2)

James 3 makes it clear that the tongue controls not only the body, but also the destiny and quality of our lives. If you could find someone whose speech was perfectly true, you'd have a perfect person, in perfect control of life.

A bit in the mouth of a horse controls the whole horse. A small rudder on a huge ship in the hands of a skilled captain sets a course in the face of the strongest winds. A word out of your mouth may seem of no account, but it can accomplish nearly anything or destroy it! (James 3:2-5 MSG)

This may seem to be a new discovery in medical science, but the Bible has revealed this fact for thousands of years. Medical science is finally finding out what the Bible says has been true all along.

For he that will love life, and see good days, let him refrain his tongue from evil, and his lips that they speak no guile. - (1 Peter 3:10)

The first thing a doctor does when examining you is look at your tongue. When you go to God with a problem, the first thing He says is, "I see the problem. It's written all over your tongue." **The speech center is the dominion center for our lives.** Our words will make us or break us. Our words determine the boundaries of our lives. Our words can limit us or loose us. God gave Adam dominion in the beginning through the power of the spoken word and that has never changed.

By thy words thou shalt be justified, and by thy words thou shalt be condemned. (Matt. 12:37)

Jesus also gave us the classic revelation of how faith works in Mark 11:23, where He said, "Whosoever shall say … he shall have whatsoever he saith." Few people take this revelation as seriously as the Bible emphasizes.

God Touches Your Mouth To Change Your World

Anytime God wants to change someone's life, He touches their mouth. God changes lives through mouth-to-mouth resuscitation! He puts His Words in our mouth to bring life, salvation, and healing. When God wants to change a city or nation, He always touches someone's mouth. God touched Isaiah's mouth with a coal of fire and sent him to speak words that would change a nation. Those words are still changing lives today, thousands of years later! God touched Jeremiah's mouth and changed his life and a nation. The list of people that God used to change a nation goes on and on, but the most important thing is that right now, God is touching your mouth and changing your world.

Man Is A Speaking Spirit

And the Lord God formed man of the dust of the ground and breathed into his nostrils the breath of life; and man became a living soul. (Gen. 2:7)

In Genesis 2:7, the phrase, "and man became a living soul," is better translated, "a speaking spirit." God created man in His own image with the capacity to speak and communicate. The power of speech was a major distinguishing factor between the animal kingdom and man. Man was made a speaking spirit and given authority and dominion. Satan recognizes the power of spoken words and is constantly trying to get man to speak words that contaminate, defile, and destroy. A constant war is going on for airtime. Satan wants to stop the spoken Word in your personal life as well as in your city or nation.

Your Voice Is Your Deliverer

Say unto them, As truly as I live, saith the Lord, as ye have spoken in mine ears, so will I do to you. (Num. 14:28)

The story of the nation of Israel's failure to possess the Promised

Land is clearly described in Numbers 13 and 14. Everyone in these two chapters got exactly what they said. There were twelve spies sent to spy out the land and bring back a report. But two of the spies, Joshua, and Caleb, won the war of words when they said, "We are well able to possess the land." Ten of the spies came back and said, "We are not able," and they died in the wilderness. Words are your address in the spirit realm. Your words custom design and specifically shape your own future. Your speech center exercises dominion in your life.

Frame Your World with the Word

Through faith we understand that the worlds were framed by the Word of God, so that things which are seen were not made of things which do appear. (Heb. 11:3)

You often hear these words when working with prison inmates, "I have been framed." The person speaking doesn't realize how true those words really are. The truth is that everyone has been framed. Our words and the words of others have framed our world. **Faith is always made up of the spoken Word of God.**

You cannot claim a promise from God's word if you aren't sure God is offering it. You cannot boldly possess things you don't realize are available to you. If your confession is wrong, your thinking is wrong! As we speak the Word of God, it tears down, roots out, builds, and plants. God wants us to speak His words and frame the picture He has for us. He has a custom plan for each of us in Christ Jesus.

For we are his workmanship, created in Christ Jesus unto good works, which God hath before ordained that we should walk in them. (Eph. 2:10)

Building Blocks - Legos

Jesus said in Mark 11:23, "Whosoever shall say ... believe those things which he saith ... he shall have whatsoever he saith." He said believe once. He said *say, saith,* and *saith,* three times. You speaking the word is vital to faith. Faith is released or put to work by speaking. If you <u>are silent</u>, you lose by default.

In Mark 11:23, Jesus used three different Greek words to explain the speaking part of faith. The first *say* is the Greek word ***epo***, which means command. It shows the authority of the believer. The second reference to speaking that Jesus used was the word, *saith*. This word in the Greek is ***laleo***, which means to speak out, use your own voice, and be bold. The third reference to speaking is also the word, *saith*. However, this Greek word is ***lego*** which means a systematic set or discourse.

How many of you are familiar with Legos for kids? It is a toy that children play with that are actually building blocks. They construct according to the diagram or picture on the box. If you will allow me to apply this understanding of lego(s) to Mark 11:23. Jesus said, "I am giving you a lego(s) a set of building blocks that you can use to frame your world according to the picture and diagram I have given to you in the Word of God."

The Bible has given us a set of <u>lego(s) - building blocks</u> for salvation, healing, blessing, prosperity, and victory of life. Take the Word of God and build your world by putting His Word in your mouth and framing your future. Your success and usefulness in this world will be measured by the power of your confession and the commitment to hold fast to what you believe!

In other words, don't just speak the confession, be committed to God's word. God will be no bigger in you than you can confess Him to be. A spiritual law that few people recognize is that your situation and circumstances are not what determines your future. Your words and your confessions shape and determine what you are and what you will become.

Watch your confession, open your mouth, and make a confession.

But make sure your confession aligns with the word of God. Understanding that confession in Greek is *homologeo,* which means:

1. to say the same thing as another, i.e., to agree with, assent
2. to concede
   a) not to refuse, to promise
   b) not to deny

Our confession will either imprison us or set us free. Our confession is the result of our believing, and our believing is the result of our right or wrong thinking. *Kenneth E. Hagin*

~ Questions For Reflection ~

1. Take a moment and reflect on your confessions.
2. Do your confessions align to God's word or to your situation?
3. Consider the last thing that occurred in your life. Was it a result of how you framed (spoke) it?
4. Ask God to help you change your confessions if they are not in alignment with His word.

Chapter Ten
CONTINUE THE JOURNEY

Chapter Ten
CONTINUE THE JOURNEY

I have been writing this book for the last twenty-five years or so, if not longer. I honestly never thought it would be written because I stopped focusing on it and became focused on life. However, a word was spoken over me last year, and the charge was, "it's time to finish the book." God brought back the burden and the heart for this message. He directed me to my notebook, where I had begun writing the details of the book, and today what you hold in your hand or read on your digital device is the fulfillment of a prophecy.

I say to you reading this book it is important for you to understand - what God has purposed before the foundation of the world, it must come to pass. The only reason it will not be fulfilled will be because you stop it. Your doubt will stop it, your silence will stop it. The perspective you have of yourself will stop it. God is not a man that He can lie, nor the son of man that He should repent (Numbers 23:19). God has purpose for you that was placed in your DNA when you were born.

As I chronicled my journey of silence for many years. Today I present to you a man who operates in boldness which comes from accepting and believing what God told me over forty-five years ago. He directed me to Revelation 10:11 and told me this was the mandate on my life.

> ***And he said unto me, Thou must prophesy again before many peoples, and nations, and tongues, and kings.***

I understand why the devil was trying to silence me. Because in my mouth was a word of liberation, deliverance, and victory. At ages twelve through eighteen I remember God pressing upon me to read and study His word, even when I was disenchanted with the church and church people. I remember God admonishing me out of Revelation 10:9

> ***And I went unto the angel, and said unto him, Give me the little book. And he said unto me, Take it, and eat it up; and it shall make thy belly bitter, but it shall be in thy mouth sweet as honey.***

There was an insatiable appetite for God's word that I couldn't shake or run from. What God was doing was putting His word in me, so I would have a reason to open my mouth because I had something to say! He said I would speak to nations. I have preached in over twenty-five states, Canada, South Africa, and the West India's, and because God's word cannot return void, I'm not done!

I wrote this book for every man who has been silenced by the vicissitudes of life… men, **don't let your silence kill you. Use it to reveal you**! You are a great man of valor like Gideon, but you don't know it yet.

The account of Gideon begins in Judges 6. From the outset, he is depicted as a man whose fear was greater than his faith. The same was true of his fellow countrymen. For seven years, they had lived in perpetual dread of the bordering Midianites and Amalekites, who repeatedly raided Israel's land, destroying their crops and stealing their livestock. Weary of hiding in caves in the mountains, the Israelites finally cried out to the Lord for help.

But look who God would send as help, Gideon. The fact that the Lord selected Gideon as the answer to deliver Israel seems strange. Why would God choose a man who was silenced by fear and intimidation – **it was proof that God's power cannot be limited even by the most unlikely human instrument**.

I was an unlikely human instrument; you may look at yourself and say the same. But when God places His hand on you, every weakness must submit to His will.

When we first meet Gideon, he is hiding from the Midianites, attempting to covertly thresh wheat in a winepress (Judges 6:11). Look at this, the process of beating out grain and separating it from the chaff normally took place out in the open, on a hilltop, where the breeze would blow the chaff away. But fearful that enemy marauders might spot him, Gideon took cover in the quarried shelter of a winepress.

Where are you hiding, my brother? Are you still hiding behind the excuse of your father not being in the home? Are you hiding behind the incarceration, ashamed that you have a criminal record? Are you hiding behind the fact you didn't finish high school and are too embarrassed to get your General Education Diploma (GED)? Well, just as the Angel of the Lord suddenly appeared to Gideon to recruit him, to enlist him, to show him who he was. So have I been sent, with a pen in my hand and a bullhorn at my mouth!

Like Gideon, who tried to rationalize if the Lord was really with them, then why did He allow all the calamity to happen? You are doing the same thing brother… that is why you've been silent this long… you've gotten stuck in your own head with your own thoughts. My assignment is to speak new thoughts and possibilities in your world.

As the Angel appeared and called Gideon out of his name – to shake up his perspective of himself, I've come to call you out of your name. Your name is not coward any longer, neither is it failure. It's a new name, Mighty Man of Valor.

Now I don't know who you are personally, and I may never set eyes on you. But that is not really important. What is important is God is calling you today.

Gideon was not only surprised by the appearance of the Angel, but it was also what the Angel said. The Angel spoke to him and said, "The Lord is with you, O valiant warrior." (Judges 6:12) Gideon denies that he is a man of bravery and tells the Angel why. "O Lord, how shall I deliver Israel? Behold my family is the least in Manasseh, and I am the youngest in my father's house."

My brother, this is what I want you to see – **the Angel of the Lord was not referring to what Gideon was, but what he would become by the strength that God provided.** Thus, He said to Gideon, "Surely I will be with you, and you shall defeat Midian as one man" (v. 16).

That is what I've come to tell you, my brother – the Lord has come to redeem your time and release you from the bondage of silence. What is amazing also about the story of Gideon is that it was the Lord Himself who came to release Gideon. What God predestined Gideon for was so serious that He came to get him directly.

My brother God cares about you in that same manner. That is why He charged me to come and get you.

My brother God summons you today to get up, wash your face, square your shoulders back, **open your mouth and break the silence!** Remember, as our parents used to say, "a closed mouth don't get fed."

PRAYER

Father God, according to Isaiah 61:1, the Spirit of the Lord God that you placed upon me, having anointed, and commissioned me to bring good news to the humble and afflicted; Father you sent me to bind up (the wounds of) the brokenhearted, to proclaim release (from confinement and condemnation) to the (physical and spiritual) captives and freedom to prisoners, (AMP)

According to your word, I speak to every brother reading this book. May the healing process begin. Healing of their emotions, healing of their self-esteem, healing of their identity. I declare, according to 2 Corinthians 10:5 imaginations, and every high thing that has exalted itself against the knowledge of God and caused my brothers to walk in shame, rejection, embarrassment, and silence be broken. I speak their thoughts, dreams and aspirations held hostage by silence be released. I declare my brothers to dream again, feel again, see again and rejoice again.

Father, the consuming anger that controlled them and surfaced as violence, introversion, perversion, and self-destruction be destroyed. Give these brothers new passions, Christ-centered desires, and peace that passeth their understanding.

I pray the repeated cycle of depression, low self-esteem and negative confession be replaced with affirming words from wives, girlfriends, mothers, mentors, and pastors. I pray their self-talk be healed and words of negativity and regret be exchanged for self-love, positivity, and expectancy.

Rename your sons and clarify their identity and put a word in their mouths to speak. I pray every vulnerability created because of word curses and failures be washed away by your word. **In the name of the Lord Jesus Christ I pray and IT IS SO!**

~ Questions For Reflection ~

1. Take a moment and reflect. What areas of your life has this book spoken to? Challenged?
2. What changes will you make today about your silence?
3. Are you determined to become who God calls you to be?

WHAT IS YOUR STRATEGY FOR CHANGE?

ABOUT THE AUTHOR

Anthony (Tony) Xaiver Page

Tony is a native Washingtonian who enjoys meeting new people and traveling the country. He is the proud father of two adult daughters: Alexandria Taylor Shields and Rhylan Cecil Page, and a doting Gee Paw of twin grandchildren: Jackson & Jamisyn Shields.

Tony has a Bachelor of Science in Pastoral Leadership, and an Associate Degree in Christian Education. He serves as Lead Pastor at Face2Face Worship Center in Clinton, Maryland, and is a Certified Relationship Counselor, HTA. Tony has served in various capacities of ministry for over 30 years. His passion is helping people identify and fulfill their purpose.

FOR BOOKINGS & CONFERENCES:

Email: <u>Pastortony@f2fwc.org</u>

Email: <u>Admin@f2fwc.org</u>

Website: <u>https://www.f2fwc.org/Anthony X. Page</u>

REFERENCES

CHAPTER ONE:

https://sbtreatment.com/blog/men-and-emotions-the-importance-of-becoming-vulnerable/

CHAPTER FOUR:

https://www.psychiatry.org/patients-families/dissociative-disorders/what-are-dissociative-disorders/

CHAPTER FIVE:

Lawrence J. Crabb, Jr. Ph.D. (1995). *The Silence of Adam...Becoming Men of Courage in A World of Chaos*

CHAPTER SEVEN:

https://www.rightattitudes.com/2008/10/04/7-38-55-rule-personal-communication/

RESOURCES:

https://fathers4kids.com/

https://www.fatherhood.org/

https://fathersrightsmovement.us/

http://blackfathersfoundation.org/

https://mankindproject.org/men-helping-men/

Made in the USA
Columbia, SC
08 July 2024